Reader's Comment

"Content excellent and easy to read. Right on with technology and wish list for home office."

Charlie Roy, Entrepreneur, Essex, CT

"...the way you present (ideas) makes one want to set up a whole new business plan. The use of humor to make a point makes the book much more readable."

Lillian Harkenrider, Longwood, FL

"*Income Surfing* is a very easy book to read--upbeat and to the point. It offers a good basic outline to follow for any business to undertake. I am on my way to being a successful *Income Surfer*!"

Rita Laverture, Business Owner, Bristol, CT

"*Income Surfing*, a neat title for an exceedingly readable book. How refreshing to read a practical guide. I read the book over the space of two nights between 10 p.m. and midnight. The book must be good to keep my interest at that hour!"

Paula Zinchoff, Business Owner, Casselberry, FL

"Well laid out--good sequencing--great use of visual graphics--easy on the eyes. Very positive message peppered with reality checks and vision."

Barry Foster, Entrepreneur, Higganum, CT

"*Income Surfing* provides an insightful look into the business world of the future. It was quick, easy reading and certainly laid out the methodology for financial survival in the 21st Century."

William Ehler, Retired U.S. Air Force, Vernon, CT

"Your predictions for the 21st century are on the money!"

Amy Lindberg, Insurance Broker, Avon, CT

"*Income Surfing* is a great book and a fresh idea that I have not seen in years. It details the way many individuals will be making money in the very near future and should become the cornerstone for consultants and trainers for this truly unique money maker you call *Income Surfing*."

David Pena, Home Based Business Support Network, Entrepreneur, Consultant, Avon, CT

"I enjoyed reading *Income Surfing*--what a marvelous concept. It was easy to catch your enthusiasm. Thought provoking, educational, and stimulating! Thanks for providing me with the insight to be proactive, taking the positive action to heighten my income potential."

Judith Kirk, Business Owner, Plainville, CT

"Overall this is one of the 10 best personal development books that I have read. It combines the wisdom of the masters with the reality of today to develop a logical vision of the 21st century. It was definitely a book I couldn't put down."

Gene Gillis, Business Owner, Avon, CT

"The information presented is definitely applicable to life and, if followed, the *Income Surfing* philosophy can change a person's life."

John Collins, President, CEO Hartford Toner and Cartridge, Inc., East Windsor, CT

"We often hear about the importance of corporate and general investment diversification. Bob Brewster and Ken Norman's compelling *Income Surfing* concept highlights the importance of multiple career income streams to reduce risk and increase wealth potential."

Bill Kenney, Owner of Grey Matter Group, LLC, The Small Business Network, Hartford, CT

INCOME SURFING©

The *New* Way to Get Rich!

The
EAGLE TEAM PUBLISHING
Group

Ellington, Connecticut USA

EAGLE TEAM BOOKS
Published by Eagle Team Publishing
The I. S. Worldwide Group, 23 Kibbe Road, Ellington, CT 06029 USA

This material has been compiled and produced by Robert O. Brewster and Kenneth G. Norman.

PUBLISHER'S NOTE
This publication is designed to provide accurate and authoritative information in regard to the subject matter covered. It is sold with the understanding that the publisher is not engaged in rendering accounting or other professional service. If expert assistance is required, the service of a competent professional person should be sought.

FOR INFORMATION, address The Eagle Team Publishing Group, 23 Kibbe Road, Ellington, CT 06029.

THE LIBRARY OF CONGRESS HAS CATALOGUED THE PAPERBACK AS FOLLOWS:
Brewster, Robert O.
Income surfing: The new way to get rich/Robert O. Brewster and Kenneth G. Norman
p. cm.
Includes bibliographical references.
ISBN 1-892044-00-5 (pbk.)
ISBN 1-892044-01-3 (hc.)
1. New business enterprises 2. Self-employed 3. Success in business
I. Norman, Kenneth A. II. Title
Library of Congress Catalog Card Number: 98-92871

Edited and proofread by Roberta J. Buland

Printed in the United States of America
Set in Times Roman
Designed by Birddog Productions

Permission to teach classes based upon this book reserved by the authors. For information regarding classes, training videos or audiotapes based upon this book, contact:

The I.S. Worldwide Group
23 Kibbe Road
Ellington, CT 06029
(860) 872-3804

Dedication

We dedicate this book…to people everywhere who tried, failed, then succeeded by never giving up…to all the people who believe that life offers unlimited opportunities to anyone with an open mind and a willingness to learn…and to everyone who wants to look back at life without regret where they never have to say…

"Should have, could have, would have … but I didn't!"

We all have two choices. We can make a living or we can design a life.

--Jim Rohn[1]

[1] Jim Rohn is recognized as America's foremost business philosopher and heads Jim Rohn International, a diversified corporation engaged in worldwide marketing and personal development, management, and sales-orientated seminars and training programs.

CONTENTS

LIST OF FIGURES

ACKNOWLEDGMENTS

Books are written for many purposes. Some are for entertainment, some are for education, while others are inspirational. Some books motivate while others create awareness. Still others are for recognition.

This book has a little bit of all of these and is a reflection of not only our thoughts and experiences, but perhaps more importantly it also reflects what we have learned from and observed in other people.

At the top of our thank you list are our spouses, Ruth and Linda, who are the best members of our team. Their encouragement for this project helped us through the challenging times. To others in our family, we extend a very special thank you, especially Stew and Donna Brewster and Joyce and Nick Scarlatelli.

Heartfelt thanks go to all the people who believe in us and the message we are conveying through this book. They provided invaluable support through their ideas, critical comments and positive attitudes.

A big thank you must go to Roberta Buland. Her professional editing and proofreading expertise helped to make the *Income Surfing* message more understandable and ultimately more powerful for the reader.

A special thank you to our investors, especially to Jim and Jean Walkenhurst, Jerome and Karen Jacobson, Al Noyes, and P.T. Davis who have given us the necessary financial support to bring *Income Surfing* to the rest of world.

PREFACE

The 21st century will not allow *anyone* to keep working in a "business as usual" manner. To achieve more than a mediocre survival will require a *new thinking--a new way of focusing*--and anyone accepting these changes will be carried to a level of success far surpassing those people who choose to remain at the status quo.

Our discovery of *Income Surfing* was no accident. We paid a big price. In fact it took a collective fifty years of research before we knew what it was and how to find it. Once discovered, it has become a life-altering phenomenon and a source of great power for us. *Income Surfing*, properly applied, can result in exciting financial and lifestyle returns.

For the average person who has above average desire, *Income Surfing* has the potential of being the greatest individual wealth-builder of all time. Some people have already harnessed its power without realizing what it is. The majority of people are still looking for it. Our goal is to make *Income Surfing* a household phrase that is synonymous with freedom of time and financial independence.

For us, the authors, our incomes over the years have been derived from a variety of businesses related to the environment, real estate, finance, consulting, nutrition, telecommunications, publishing and transportation. Although not always planned, these income sources seem to naturally complement each other and fit into our desire to maximize our time and talents.

During a discussion about the rapidly changing times and the approaching millennium, we discovered that what we had been doing for many years might be something that other people could or would want to do *if they knew about it*. In our lectures we frequently talked about "multiple source income bases." An earlier book, *Never Sleep Again* written in 1992 by Bob Brewster, explains this approach as a way to become wealthy. The question was also raised: could this method of making money become a philosophy or a new movement for acquiring wealth? If so, what do we name earning money from many different sources *at the same time*?

To us, it was clear that changing times are dictating a new way of thinking and what we have been doing could be, for many people, an important key to the 21st century. But, again, what about a name? Then we had a revelation. Had not *channel surfing* with the remote control revolutionized television? Why not *Income Surfing*? It had already changed our lives. Why couldn't it forever change how people earned money? The television remote control has eliminated *non-productive* commercial-watching time. Couldn't *Income Surfing* eliminate *non-productive* income-earning time?

As you read about our discovery, look at it as *your* discovery also. Put yourself in our position and think about how *Income Surfing* could change your life forever. You *already* have the skills and talent. You *already* have the knowledge. Hopefully you are *already* motivated, but if you are not we know you will be once you understand what *Income Surfing* can accomplish for you.

First let us set the scene for your coming discovery. Hollywood! Movies! Television! Professional Sports! Newspapers! Magazines! Radio! Tabloids!

Where is the reality? It is getting harder to tell real life from fiction. Young people are especially finding it harder to tell the difference as the line grows grayer and good role models become more difficult to identify. The good life is not an overnight success story. It is hard work. It is persistence with a plan and goals. As a people, the surrealistic world of film and television has clouded our sense of reality and is causing us to expect more before we have even gotten started or paid a price.

In the real world, the truth is that more can be accomplished today than ever before in history, *if* we have the patience and understanding to grow and develop personally to handle the success. We must also be realistic about the success we want to achieve. You do not have to be a millionaire to live like one. You just have to know a few simple facts and follow the rules. In this book we spell out the rules and help you understand how to play by them.

No one said that life was going to be easy! There is always a price that must be paid. On the other hand we ask, "Must life be hard in order to reach success?" We believe that success can be achieved by having fun, where you are in control, and where you understand that your attitude means...*life is not what you make of it, it's how you take it.* What seems to elude most people is the ability to have fun while becoming successful. We believe that *Income Surfing* provides the way to get all you can out of life and have fun, too!

The end of the 20th century is creating havoc with traditional thinking. Job security is a thing of the past. Working for one company in a lifelong career is no longer the norm nor is it secure. Graduation to grave days are gone forever. Job turmoil has arrived and will continue for a long time. That's the bad news. So where is the future? That's the good news!

At no time has there been a greater opportunity to jump ahead in life than right now. To gain a perspective on this statement we need to look back over 100 years. In 1896, people flocked from all over the world to Alaska's Yukon Territory when the word spread of a major gold discovery. A small group of men had emerged from the Yukon near Nome with millions of dollars in gold dust and set off what would become a stampede of people wanting to become rich. As soon as the news hit the street, people all over North America dropped whatever they were doing, packed a few things and started what would become for many a fruitless journey to make their fortune. Tens of thousands of these people had no experience in finding gold and living in the wilderness. Nevertheless, they went anyway. It was mass hysteria and chaos. Hundreds died on the trail from exhaustion or exposure. Even if they made it to the gold fields, it took extreme efforts to stake a claim, prospect it, and then protect it, if gold was ever found. Success was reserved for those who properly prepared, who were teachable and who had a burning desire to succeed. For them their success would be life-altering.

Today, we have our own stampede, but instead of gold we are now rushing to create independent business incomes from our small offices and home offices (SOHO). It has been predicted that by the year 2,005 over 50% of all goods and services will be purchased from the home. This trend is creating a massive opportunity to build a business without the traditional overhead and associated liabilities that plague the majority of businesses. Yet, like the people who sought gold in 1896, success will be reserved for the few who prepare, who are teachable and who have a burning desire to succeed today.

Similar to our gold rush ancestors who looked for gold to create momentum in the 20th century, our success today will actually be creating momentum for the 21st century. The "Big Money" will go to those who get positioned now. Remember, history has taught us a valuable lesson. When times are the most confusing, the chances to get ahead are at their greatest. This happens because most people will stand around watching in a state of indecision. This creates a period where competition is minimal. By taking action now you are creating an advantage that can propel you over those who may have more money and/or more talent--past those who hesitate or wait. This is your chance to jump ahead...become an *Income Surfer*...and change your life forever!

Hooray for today...hooray for the future!!

Bob Brewster and Ken Norman

> **There is one thing stronger than all the armies in the world, and that is an idea whose time has come.**
>
> --Victor Hugo

INCOME SURFING©

The *New* Way to Get Rich!

Chapter 1

WHO WE ARE

> **If you want to know how rich you really are, find out what would be left of you tomorrow if you should lose every dollar you own tonight.**
>
> --William J. H. Boetcker[2]

Perhaps we should be asking, "Who are you?" We already know who we are, but do you know who you are? If you are like us, you are ambitious, smart and confident. You want more from life, desire money, want to be loved and to love, need to be appreciated, seek recognition and strive for happiness.

Would it surprise you if you were told that money is the chief cause of domestic disputes and that it contributes to the majority of divorces and business breakups? Where do you put money on your list of priorities? Think about your answer. Is money always on your mind, or do you think about it only occasionally?

---

[2] William Boetcker, The Forbes Book of Business Quotations, NY: Black Dog & Levanthal Publishers, Inc., 1997, page 888

Most people think about financial matters most of the time. They creep into most decisions. They drive most actions. They cause us to do things we normally would not do and that is from both sides--having too much money as well as not having enough.

A recent study listed those events that have the greatest impact on our lives. In order of importance they are listed in Figure 1 shown below.

Figure 1. Social Adjustment Rating Scale

Rank	Life Event	Points
1.	Death of spouse..................................	100
2.	Divorce..	73
3.	Marital separation...............................	65
4.	Jail Term..	63
5.	Death of close family member..................	63
6.	Personal injury or illness........................	53
7.	Marriage...	50
8.	Fired at work.......................................	47
9.	Marital reconciliation............................	45
10.	Retirement..	45
11.	Changes in family member's health...........	44
12.	Pregnancy...	40
13.	Sex difficulties.....................................	39
14.	Gain of new family member.....................	39
15.	Business readjustment...........................	39
16.	Change in financial status.......................	38
17.	Death of close friend.............................	37
18.	Change to different line of work................	36
19.	Change in number of arguments with Spouse	35
20.	Mortgage or loan over $10,000.................	31
21.	Foreclosure of mortgage or loan................	31
22.	Change in work responsibilities................	29
23.	Son or daughter leaving home...................	29
24.	Trouble with in-laws.............................	29
25.	Outstanding personal achievement.............	28
26.	Spouse begins or stops work....................	26

RANK	LIFE EVENT	POINTS
27.	Begin or end school	26
28.	Change in living conditions	25
29.	Revision of personal habits	24
30.	Trouble with boss	23
31.	Change in work hours, conditions	20
32.	Change in residence	20
33.	Change in schools	20
34.	Change in recreation	19
35.	Change in church activities	18
36.	Change in social activities	18
37.	Mortgage or loan under $10,000	17
38.	Change in sleeping habits	16
39.	Change in number of family gatherings	15
40.	Change in eating habits	15
41.	Vacation	13
42.	Christmas	12
43.	Minor violations of the law	11

[3]

After reviewing Figure 1, are you surprised at the fact that the first *financial*-related event is # 16? Look at the fifteen events which precede it. No wonder many of these other events occur. They are brought on by a preoccupation with financial matters that steals time from other important matters.

Who we are is not a function of financial status. Who we are is a function of how we view ourselves from a self-worth standpoint. A negative self-image will cause us to falsely blame other factors for our problems. A negative self-image will usually keep us from doing the things we need to be doing. A lack of self-confidence will lead to failures in other areas.

We should not be focused on financial matters. Our focus should be on the things we need to be doing to make our

[3] T.H. Holmes and R.H. Rahe, *Journal of Psychosomatic Research*

lives all that they can be. The ugly fact is that most people lead mediocre lives. They have allowed themselves to become average. They let other people dictate what they should do and who they should become. This is not the way to live life, and it is simply not good enough anymore.

What are you? Average? Above average? Well above average? Outstanding? If you want to live like a millionaire start thinking like one. The rest of this book will help you figure out how.

The average person puts only 25% of his energy and ability into his work. The world takes off its hat to those who put in more than 50% of their capacity, and stands on its head for those few and far between souls who devote 100%.

--Andrew Carnegie

Chapter 2

THE 21ST CENTURY

The empires of the future are the empires of the mind.

--Winston Churchill

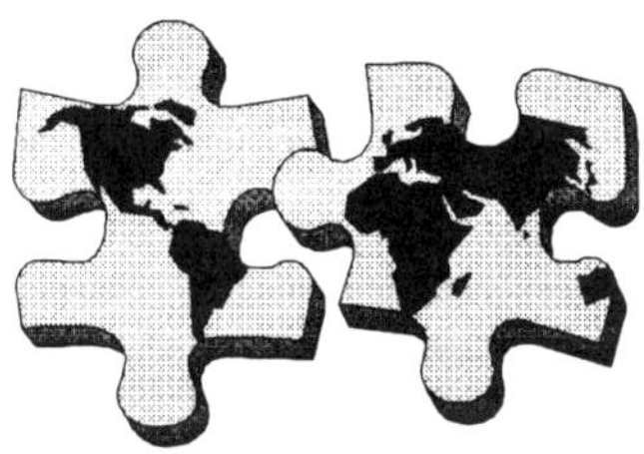

Before we go into *Income Surfing* in detail, we need to say something about the 21st century. At the time of this book printing, we really do not believe anybody knows what the early 21st century will be like, and since everyone is guessing, we thought we are taking an educated guess. Here is what we see coming in the first quarter of the 21st century.

JOBS

Most people will *not* have only *one* job. They will have many. The days of living on one income no matter what its source will be over.

SKILLS

These various jobs will require a variety of skills. No longer will people specialize in just one thing--the risk will be too high both financially and from a personal achievement standpoint.

EDUCATION

Formal education will be more important than ever. A college degree will only open the door. It will provide proof that the individual can set goals and stay with them until accomplished. The prestige of attending a top university will diminish as education becomes more general. Faculty members and administrators at institutions of higher learning will struggle to keep up with galloping trend changes and new technologies. Continued education will become more important, and individuals who maintain some form of personal growth program will lead the way to getting the best opportunities.

INCOME

This category has nothing to do with jobs. The successful person of tomorrow will derive incomes from many different sources. We call this *Income Surfing*. Each income source will be complementary and nonconflicting with the others. Each will be turned on or off. They will not all function at the same time because when one is taking off, another will be slowing down. These cycles will cause people to seek out and control anywhere from two to five income sources.

WEALTH

It is clear that there is a new breed of wealth builder developing. Unlike their predecessors who spent millions to decorate homes or to build monumental empires, this new breed will be more laid back and seek anonymity. They will want a more average appearing life with less stress and more family orientation. Under the surface, however, they will be engineering deals and transactions to create more change. They will be less apt to hoard their wealth and will be willing to take greater risks.

COMMUNICATIONS

Perhaps the fastest changing industry of all, communications will affect everyone's life. No one will escape either the good times from going up or the bad times from coming down. Those who harness its advances in their early stages

will gain the advantage over those who hesitate. Yet, those who make gains but then relax or fail to make continuous changes will fall behind and eventually be replaced. The world will shrink down to instant voice, data and visual transmissions to open up tremendous new opportunities.

HEALTH

Preventive health care will be the driving force in the health industry. Much of the research to find cures for certain diseases will slow or shift to prevention. Billions of dollars will be redirected to education, related to proper diet and the avoidance of poor health habits. People who consciously or deliberately violate good health habits or who do not practice prevention will be asked to pay a much higher share of health care costs. Life expectancy will continue to drop rather than increase because of generations of children from the 1970s, 1980s and 1990s who abused their health by smoking, drug and alcohol abuse, and eating the wrong food. According to a report released on February 29, 1996, by the U.S. Centers for Disease Control and Prevention, the general trend for improvement in life expectancy dropped for the first time since 1930.[4] This shift will create a dire situation and will accelerate education and research into prevention, creating more financial opportunities.

---

[4] Associated Press, *Hartford Courant* newspaper April 30, 1996

GOVERNMENT

Sadly, the result of general population apathy toward government in the 1980s and 1990s when less than fifty percent of the voting population turned out for major elections is leading to a diversity of splinter groups all claiming to represent the majority. Some groups will foster changes in the overall system or advocate a new system. Other groups will cut government to its simplest form and leave the majority of governing to local and state governments. Still others will want government to grow and to provide more and new services. Finally, other groups will press to set up their own government. Regardless of the choice times will be traumatic before they get better, leading to confusion, discouragement and distrust.

LEADERSHIP

The public will demand leaders who have personal integrity and honesty. It will want its leaders to have attributes that set an example for people to follow. The public will grow increasingly more disenchanted with personalities or public figures who fail to live lives by example, hold to a higher standard and be roles models for the young.

PROFESSIONAL SPORTS PEOPLE AND CELEBRITIES

Support for higher salaries and compensation packages will fail rapidly as the public demands more from these people. Public disgust will be demonstrated in fewer sales and greatly reduced promotion spending. Being a celebrity will carry a high price, and those people who exhibit behavior not becoming of a role model will not be tolerated.

CORPORATE COMPENSATION

Pay for top executives will tumble as public sentiment grows increasingly negative against excessive compensation packages.

Example teaches better than precept. It is the best modeler of the character of men and women. To set a lofty example is the richest bequest a man can leave behind him.

--Samuel Smiles[5]

[5] Samual Smiles, *The Forbes Book of Business* Quotations, page 258

Chapter 3

WHAT IS *INCOME SURFING*?

You can't escape the responsibility of tomorrow by evading it today.
--Abraham Lincoln

When we discovered *Income Surfing*, we were not specifically looking for it. However, once we found it and subsequently learned what we could do with it, our lives changed forever.

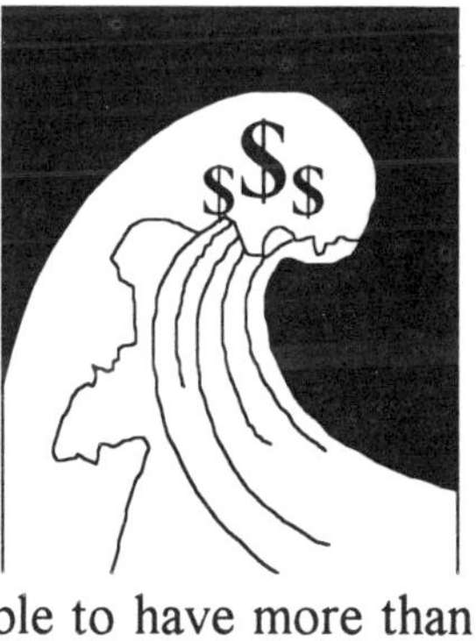

Although previously defined, we want to be absolutely sure you know what *Income Surfing* means. It is the ability to earn money from several different sources at the same time. Each source must not conflict but be complementary to the other sources. It takes a minimum of two and a maximum of five sources to *Income Surf*. (Some people may be able to have more than five sources, but they will be the rare exception.)

Before discussing some examples of *Income Surfing*, let us look at *why Income Surfing* is the future.

In the early- to mid- 20th century, it was common for one wage earner to carry the financial load for an entire family. Rarely did both spouses in a family work. After World War II the world was rebuilding itself and new economies started to boom. The opportunities to work harder and longer for higher financial gain took hold. As products and services increased in number, so did appetites for purchasing them. Credit cards and debt were more easily obtained. The good life was there for the taking with just a signature. Vacations and recreational pastimes became necessities rather than luxuries. Bigger homes and more expensive cars now consume more of our earned income. Today, one income is not enough to sustain our desires and needs.

As spending and debt have increased so has inflation and the erosion of purchasing power along with it. According to the *New York Times 1998 Almanac* each dollar earned in 1996 is worth only 15 cents compared to a dollar earned 1950.[6] Economic experts say that zero inflation is an impossibility which means that some type of erosion in purchasing power is going to occur no matter what happens. However, it is no wonder that a second income from a part-time job or from a spouse working has become necessary. The luxury of working for extra money has been replaced with the necessity to earn money just to live.

As further proof, in 1970 the average per capita income in the United States was $4,047. In 1994 it was $21,696. On the surface this looks like a five times growth rate which might seem impressive. However, as shown in Figure 2,

---

[6] *New York Times 1998 Almanac* "Purchasing Power of the Dollar 1950-1996", page 336.

when adjusting the dollar value from 1970 to 1994, incomes have only gone from $4,047 to 5,378!! [7]

Figure 2. Change in Per Capita Income 1970-94

Year	Per Capita Income	Real Income Adjusted for Inflation	Percent Change
1970	$ 4,047	----	----
1994	$21,809	$5,378	**132%**

[8]

According to the *New York Times 1998 Almanac:*

> While hourly and weekly wages (in current dollars) have more than tripled since 1970...when inflation is accounted for, real earnings (in constant [1982] dollars) have decreased steadily over the past two decades. Hourly earnings have fallen 7% since 1970, while weekly earnings have dropped nearly 14%. Thus, even though 1995 paychecks have more zeros on the end, they do not go as far as a 1970 paycheck (did) to cover living expenses. [9]

Adding a second income through additional jobs or the spouse going to work is a natural solution, but only solves the problem temporarily. The real problem is that there are only twenty-four hours in a day so creating more time is a physical impossibility. As more and more time has to be invested to earn money, other parts of life suffer. For example, the divorce rate has increased. Crime has

---

[7] *The New York Times 1998 Almanac* pages 334-336

[8] Ibid

[9] Ibid page 350

increased. Families have fallen apart. Material gain has been placed before spiritual gain. The need to make more money in ever shorter periods of time has become the driving force. And, unfortunately some people do not like working hard so they commit crimes to get ahead. The jails are full of these people who took the "easy" way out.

Fortunately, on the other hand, the majority of people want to get ahead and are willing to do it in a positive, creative fashion. In their quest for financial gain, these people are creating opportunities that employ tens of thousands of other people in whole new industries worldwide.

Franchising is a good example of this. Business franchising once looked down upon, now accounts for over one-third of the U.S. economy. Many people who have started a franchise to replace or increase an income are now wealthy and can buy more. Franchising is really a way for a person to leverage his or her time--to create more opportunity for income within a limited amount of time. It is using the "power of numbers."

Here is what *The New York Times 1998 Almanac* says about franchising:

> Franchising, a century-old tradition, has never been more popular in the United States than it is now. There were 540,000 franchised businesses in 1995, employing more than 8 million people, and doing more than $758 billion in sales. Franchised business represents nearly 40 percent of all U.S. retail sales. The Department of Commerce estimates that by the

year 2000, franchising will account for more than half of all sales."[10]

In general, business has grown enormously since World War II. During this period corporate America offered security, benefits, education and retirement--the good life! At the same time, entrepreneurial spirited businesspeople offered opportunity for workers to grow with the business and the chance to gain ownership through stock options and bonus programs. Overall, America's wealthy have grown in numbers. No longer can the term "millionaire" be reserved for a few. "Billionaire" is now starting to become the term for top income people.

Yet, in spite of the great economic gains and the undeniable gains in lifestyle, it has become increasingly clear that for many people the dream remains out of reach. For these people their day is spent locked into a job or income cycle that offers little room to grow. They have given their time to someone else. They are being bought "wholesale" and are being sold "retail." To many of these people a "job" means "just over broke." As more people gain financial independence to rise into the upper middle or wealthy class, more people in the middle class are dropping down into the lower middle class or even becoming poor.

How can this be happening in a society which supposedly offers such great opportunity? The answers are far too complex to address here but what has happened is not a plot nor was it designed by one individual or group of people. It just happened. Government has not failed nor has corporate America created this situation. The rich are not to blame, for who among us would not want to take their place? It is

---

[10] *The New York Times 1998 Almanac* page 364

not the fault of foreign competition or even labor unions. We cannot blame our education system or the educators who are working so hard with so little.

There is no one reason for our situation today. It is a by-product of evolutionary change. With every change or advancement in the world, there is a price to pay. With every good deed there is an opposite bad deed. With every two steps forward, there is often one step backwards. With every economic gain there is economic loss.

There is no question that in the 21st century, we will be better off than we are today. But we *will not* be earning money the way we do today, and here is where *Income Surfing* comes in. Tomorrow's successful people will be more flexible overall, work flexible hours, be more entrepreneurial, be less focused on one thing, be experts in several things, hold a job an average of three to five years or work as an outside contractor from project to project, enjoy family life more, be away from home less, be more worldly in thinking, use more technology and be more team-spirited.

Those of us who are already *Income Surfing* know that tomorrow's world is here today. We have seen tomorrow and love it. We are excited about our future and what we can accomplish; it is greater than the sum of our past. Through *Income Surfing* we can double, triple or even quadruple our incomes in a relatively short period of time. We can live where we choose, work when we choose, and work with whom we choose. All of our skills and talents can be used to build new ones. We can accelerate time by making time our ally instead of our enemy. We can set goals and reach them. We can become masters of our own destiny.

The best part is that as an *Income Surfer* we do not have to be a millionaire to live like one. Once you understand what *Income Surfing* is, your world will change. You will have the control of your life back, and the frustration you feel today will be gone forever.

Let us look at one example of *Income Surfing*. The person we will describe is very real. As a matter of fact, you already know who he is. His name is Bob Brewster, one this book's authors.

I have a college degree in education. I was drafted into the U.S. Army and volunteered to go to Vietnam during the war. I am a highly experienced civilian and military pilot with over 300

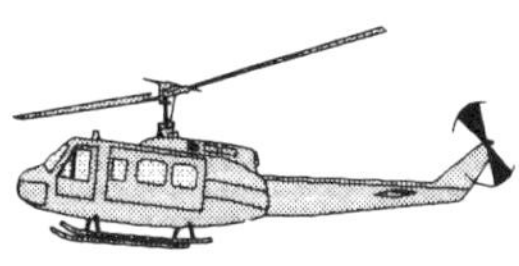

combat missions and four valor awards. I survived three aircraft crashes; in two the aircraft was totally destroyed and I escaped unhurt! I have founded over eight businesses and have been a company president four times. I have written books and lectured to groups of people. I have also been financially broke and have worked three jobs at one time to make ends meet. I have no special advantage nor was I ever given one. So why am I an example of *Income Surfing*?

In 1995, I earned exactly twice as much money as I had earned in 1994. I did this from my home office without increasing my overhead or borrowing any money. I even traveled *less*. How did I do this? I started the year earning money from a products distribution business I had been building for several years. This business was broken down into two parts--nutrition and environmental products.

Although this income was adequate, it was not growing at a pace that I found acceptable. I then decided to look at other things which I could do in and around this primary distribution business. One income source I discovered to complement my existing business was to earn money from the sale of gold bullion coins. I also learned that there were many rapidly growing opportunities in the telecommunications industry. In addition, I realized that my aviation background provided a unique expertise that could help other aviation businesses so I promoted myself as an aviation consultant.

Figure 3 shows how my income broke down according to percentages of earnings. This is an actual example of *Income Surfing* accomplished in one year based on a course direction achieved over several years. The types of incomes and the timing to achieve them will vary from one person to another. Following one of Stephen Covey's principles for *The Seven Habits of Highly Effective People* which is *begin with an end in mind*[11], you can accomplish the same thing. Remember, your goal is to be time and financially independent. Your time is worth more than your money. *Income Surfing* treats time as a precious resource—a non-renewable resource.

As you look at Figure 3, think of yourself and replace the incomes I experienced with the ones you would like to develop over a period of time.

---

[11] Stephen R. Covey, *The Seven Habits of Highly Effective People,* NY: Simon & Shuster Audio Division.

Figure 3. *Income Surfing* Example

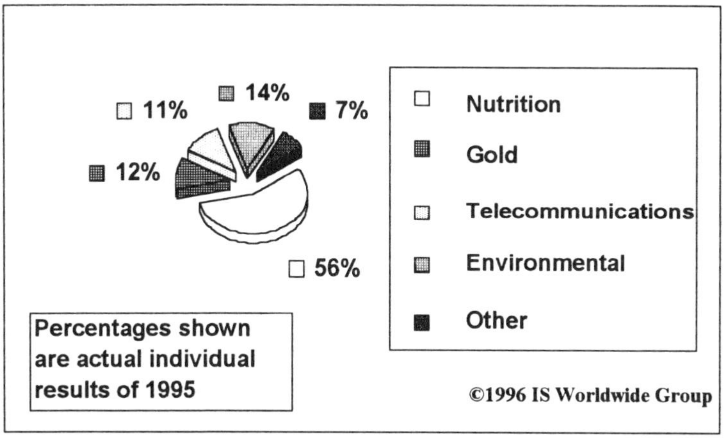

[12]

From Figure 3 it is evident that I earned money from five different sources which varied in percentages of the total income from 7 percent to 56 percent. What is interesting to note is that the sources of income did not conflict with each other. They could all be turned on at one time. A clear fact of life is that everything we do does not run at its maximum all the time. With *Income Surfing* when one income is idling or slowing down, another income is accelerating. The goal is to keep the overall *total income* growing at a rate that exceeds what could be done with any one source by itself.

The advantages of *Income Surfing* are obvious. Dependence on one source of income is eliminated. This freedom not only eliminates the trauma associated with losing one source of income, but it also frees up the individual to invest time where and when it has the greatest return. Done properly,

[12] The I.S. Worldwide Group was founded in 1995 by Bob Brewster and Ken Norman to study and promote the multiple source income philosophy.

Income Surfing can be accomplished with only a little more effort than working at one single income source but with a financial return many times greater. How you manage yourself will be a key factor in your success.

The next figure of "The Successful Person in the 21st Century" is representative of what people will be doing. The various income sources will of course vary from person to person but the overall tactics and strategy will be similar.

Figure 4. Successful Person in the 21st Century

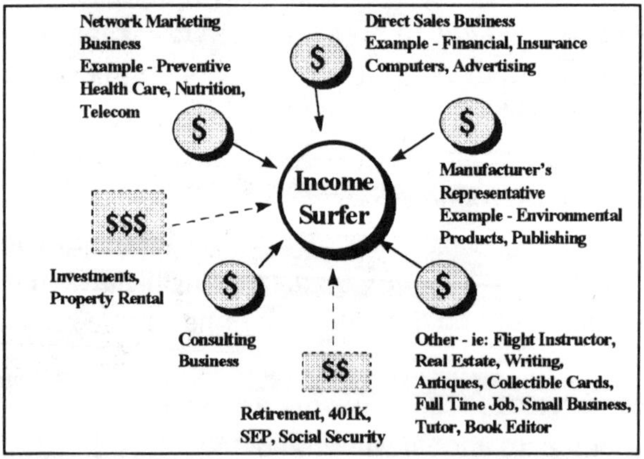

Wow!!
This *Income Surfing* is a Great Way to Make Big $$$!!!!

Chapter 4

WHY *INCOME SURFING* IS A TREND

> **If you use the current trends as a reference point, you'll be able to interpret things with an eye toward making trend connections on your own.**
>
> --Faith Popcorn[13]

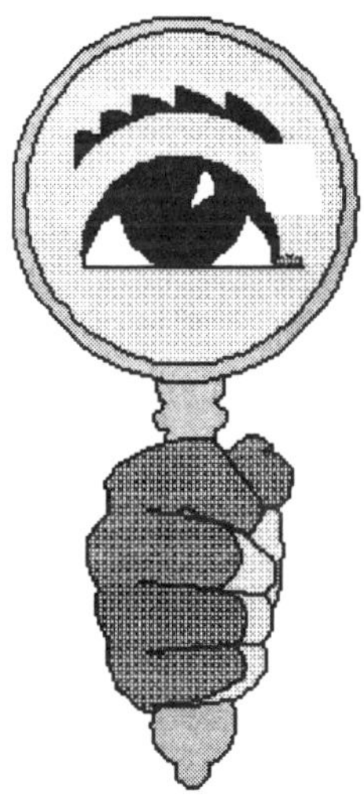

The 21st century will operate under different employment rules than those in force in the 20th century. How prepared you are for these new rules will determine how well you succeed.

There are many driving forces behind these new employment trends.

MORE COMPETITION

As the work force continues to downsize and job security becomes less and less common, the number of skilled and experienced workers looking for a job will increase. But, there will be fewer jobs,

[13] Faith Popcorn, *The Popcorn Report*, NY: Bantam Doubleday Dell Publishing, 1991, Page 180.

and upward mobility will decrease. The overall effect will give employers an advantage when looking for the best people to hire.

JACK-OF-ALL-TRADES

The workplace will operate at a faster pace. More jobs will be based on performance, and the worker will have to be skilled in several functions. Because the work force will be smaller, each person will handle more responsibilities. Flexibility in job function will be the key to individual success. The workday will be longer and there will be less time off for holidays and on weekends.

RESPONSIVENESS

The faster workplace pace will force workers to be quicker thinkers and better decision makers. Emphasis will be placed on getting more out of less and in developing a more refined expertise.

COMPUTERESE

Computers will be everywhere and everyone will be expected to have basic computer skills. Software programs will exist for almost every function. The Internet will affect everyone's position because of accessibility and easily obtained information. E-mail will be standard for everyone. Technology will be continuously and rapidly changing requiring that people constantly upgrade their skills and accept ever changing job functions.

EXPERIENCE PAYS

Older, experienced workers will have an advantage. Compared to new hires or college graduates, they will require higher compensation or benefits but will be more reliable and less costly to train.

INDEPENDENT WORKERS

The trend for outsourcing work will grow faster. There will be more contract and consulting work. College graduates will find it harder to get a job in their respective fields and will need to accept employment in other areas while they work into their degree-required career.

LONGER WORK DAYS

Workers will be asked to put in longer days. Non-traditional work schedules will pose the question, "Which 12 hours do you want to work?" Dress attire will become more casual. Cultural diversity will be more common in the workplace. Schedules will become more family oriented.

SOLO DAYS GONE

The requirement to be a team player will replace individualism because more accountability and responsibility will be needed to reach all management levels.

SELLING YOURSELF

Selling yourself will become a very important skill. Each job or project will require individual promotion of skills and experiences as companies and government agencies increasingly utilize outside self-employed and more entrepreneurial individuals in place of dedicated employees.

PERFORM OR ELSE

Performance-based pay and incentives will drive compensation rewards. Fewer benefits will be offered as workers put in more hours for less pay.

FREE AS A BIRD

Workers will be more mobile and flexible in finding jobs across a broader geographical area. Career moves will become more frequent.

HAVE BRIEFCASE, WILL TRAVEL

The change in the world economy and the shrinking of the world through technology and communications may mean a more global-hopping work force as jobs change definition.

THE CUSTOMER COMES FIRST

Increased service to the customer will drive the market as new methods are found to streamline customer service and enhance company responsiveness. Ineffective overheads will be eliminated. The resulting smaller work force will be better appreciated by the employer as positive customer acceptance grows.

WORK AT HOME

More work will be done from home. Corporate physical plants will shift from office-based to more manufacturing-based as the employee shift to more flexible work arrangements gains momentum.

In summary, the need for individuals to take control of their own destinies will dictate how people invest their time. *Income Surfing* will become the norm as people learn that they can accomplish more for themselves with proper self-discipline, good time management and the right attitude.

SELF DISCIPLINE,
GOOD TIME MANAGEMENT
THE RIGHT ATTITUDE!

Chapter 5

CONTROLLING OFFICE EXPENSES AS AN INCOME SURFER

> **Money is a terrible master but an excellent servant.**
>
> --P. T. Barnum

As *Income Surfers,* we have learned a powerful rule for the money we make. *It is not what you earn, it is what you keep.*

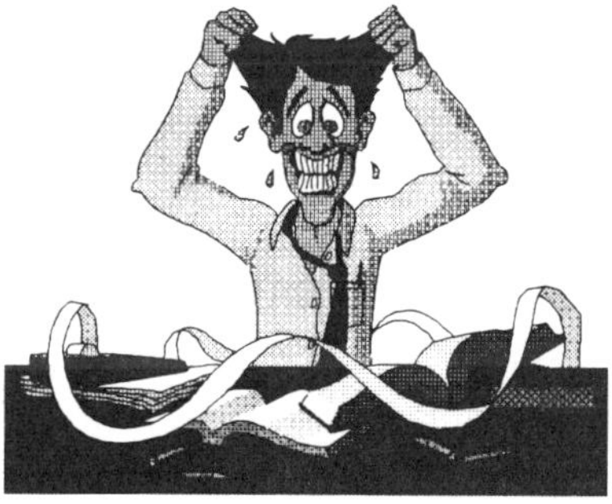

We are being bombarded with every imaginable way to spend our money. Although it is only natural to spend the money you earn, it is also very wise to spend it on things you *really* need.

Converting from a traditional business mentality to a home business mentality can be a major leap for most people. The belief that overhead must be similar can lead to a serious problem. Do not fall into this trap. The difficulty of cutting expenses and overhead once it has been established has already proved to be an anguishing experience for big business and should be a key lesson for us in our home businesses.

A home business should be kept simple. This does not mean that you will only work with paper and pencil. On the contrary, today most sophisticated home businesses have capabilities that rival their big brother counterparts. Experience has shown that a home office can be capable of doing everything that a major company can do. In addition, because of size and closer control the home office should offer more efficiency for the use of time and materials.

It was not too long ago that facsimile machines were found in only 5 percent of larger size businesses. Today over 90 percent of traditional businesses have a fax. Homes are following the same trend. Today about 5 percent of homes have a fax machine, but the number is growing rapidly as technology advances.

When you start a home business, be willing to spend money to make sure it is done right. However, the key is to be very selective about what you spend your money on. Be sure that you cannot do something better and at less cost outside your home office. Many office services can be purchased from people who specialize in them. Before we could afford a quality laser printer, we did all our presentation printing at a local office services business which provided a wide variety of work stations and equipment. In addition, this type of outside service usually offers the use of the latest software, computers and printers. Since most office services businesses charge by the minute or hour, we often do the majority of the creative work in our home office on our own equipment. This keeps expenses to a minimum.

Another business we used a lot was local office products stores. Many of these have a national presence making it easy to find familiar services when traveling. They not only sell all types of paper and office products, but they also provide self-service copy machines at a low cost. Purchase the paper in packs of 500 sheets at a low cost, go to their self-serve copiers or assisted copy center, and at minimum cost produce good quality materials.

Later in this chapter there are more specific hints about office equipment. To help you get started and become more efficient, the following tips will be useful in establishing your home office.

DO NOT BE A CHEAPSKATE

Buying cheap equipment will ultimately cost you more, and whatever you produce will look cheap. If you can afford it, purchase a laser printer up front. The image you will present will more than earn you enough money to offset the extra cost. If you are doing color work, look for a good photo quality color printer.

GET A FAX MACHINE

Not owning a fax machine will cost you more money in time spent running around. With the price of gas and car costs rising, whatever you can do to prevent taking extra trips will save a lot of money over time. Besides, fax machines are becoming standard equipment everywhere.

GET ON THE INTERNET

Either subscribe to an on-line service with Internet access or subscribe directly to an Internet Service Provider (ISP). Available resources and the information you gather will propel you years ahead of others who ignore this rapidly growing business tool.

PUT YOUR FINANCIAL INFORMATION ON A COMPUTER

Do not be stubborn and attempt to track your financial matters manually. For all but a few, those days are gone forever. There are excellent financial software programs available which are user-friendly. You just plug in the numbers. The program allows you to track all your accounts, easily balance them, budget expenses, and make forecasts. Best of all when tax time comes, you can print out a variety of reports with all your expenditures neatly categorized for your accountant. Using a financial software program has been one of our best time-savers and has helped us efficiently balance accounts. It may also be invaluable to track payments if you need to recreate an account history or research a payment that someone disputes.

GROW INTO THE EQUIPMENT YOU NEED

Do not attempt to purchase everything in one day. Obtain equipment as the need dictates. This way you avoid wasting money on things that look exciting but are not practical for you.

CONTROL YOUR EXPENSES

Make an effort to establish cost controls that are easy to follow. For example, keep a box of scrap paper handy. Use this paper that is blank on one side to print draft letters or proposals, saving the good paper for the final printing. You can also use this paper for notepads by cutting it into different sizes and stapling it together. Recycle laser printer cartridges instead of buying new ones each time they run out. Shop around for a long-distance carrier that offers you one rate for 24-hours seven-day calling and who bills you in six-second or less increments rather than by the minute. (Do not be fooled by the big name companies. They often charge the highest rates.)

ANSWER YOUR PHONES PROFESSIONALLY

Make sure you have an efficient and professional sounding phone message system. Nothing is a greater turnoff then calling a business number and hearing a message by a young child or an unprofessional voice. Music in the background and an excessively long (over 20 seconds) or unintelligible message will cause callers to hang up. Be sure your message system offers remote retrieval so that you can make timely responses while away from your office. Some telephone companies offer a service that takes messages when you are on the line. This professional service helps avoid busy signals and allows for the retrieval of messages as soon as a call is ended.

SET UP SEPARATE BUSINESS PHONE LINES

The cost of separate phone lines is well worth it. We have one line and answer machine for the family. Our home office has a separate fax line and two business lines. We operate our computer modem through the same line as our fax machine.

AVOID UNNECESSARY BACKGROUND NOISES

Make sure that you have no background noise when you are speaking on the phone. Noisy children, barking dogs or a television playing in the background can be disruptive to your caller and detract from conducting a businesslike conversation in a professional manner.

BE TOUGH ON GETTING PAID

If there is one lesson we learned the hard way, it was the need to establish a billing policy for services we rendered so that we would get paid in a timely fashion. As a small business with little to no cash reserve, cash flow was critical. When we started asking for partial or whole payment up front, at first it was difficult. But as we grew and fewer people objected, it has minimized the impact of slow or no payers. If you can afford it, set up your checking account with a hidden reserve to cover those times when your cash may run low. Many banks offer overdraft protection also. Using this reserve usually happens when a payment that was promised fails to arrive. We keep an extra few thousand dollars in our account even though our accounting program shows the balance as zero.

DEVELOP A BUSINESS POLICY

Spell out rules to friends, neighbors and family so that they know you are conducting a business and are not available for socializing.

PRESENT YOURSELF PROFESSIONALLY

All of your presentation materials from business cards to brochures should be very professional. Do not be cheap. It will show. Treat these items as if they were your employees hired to work for you. You would want them at their best professional dress and presentation form. And, if you do it right, you will not have to hire employees, one of the biggest headaches in business!

DO NOT FORGET THAT YOU ARE IN BUSINESS

Make sure that mowing the lawn does not prevent you from sending out that proposal letter. Make a list of priorities and stick to it. Complete a "To Do" list for the next day so when you go to bed at night you will already know what the next morning's activities will be. Tasks that are directly related to making money should take priority over everything else. On the other hand, when it is time for personal or family affairs, turn the business "off." As a rule, we answer the business phone even when it is "after hours," if we are not busy. It costs less to answer a call than to make a return call, and when we do answer late, many callers are "surprised that we are still working" thus creating a better image of our business for them.

JOIN PROFESSIONAL GROUPS AND ASSOCIATIONS

Get out and network. Do not be an isolationist. You need to interact with others and let them know what you do. Watch the newspapers for seminars and meetings that you can attend. This interaction will not only help you grow personally but the contacts you make will keep your mind sharp. Keep a few brochures in your pocket. Never, never, ever leave home without your business cards. The one time you do not have them you will meet a key contact that could be your next client or customer, and you will be fumbling for something credible to give them. Use business networking groups to practice your marketing ideas. Their reactions will help you decide whether or not you should continue using your idea.

EXERCISE YOUR BODY

Make sure you have a regular exercise program. If you are not in an organized program offered by a health or fitness club, be sure to create your own routine and stick to it each day. Physical fitness and mental alertness go hand in hand.

TAKE CARE OF YOUR PERSONAL HEALTH

Water and air problems are growing rapidly. If you are connected to a municipally treated water supply, add a filter to your system. Even though chlorine is necessary for safe water, there is much credible evidence for filtering it out before using it. In addition filtering your own water is cheaper than buying bottled water. Filter the air in your office. Accumulated gases and stale air create fatigue. These gases come from your office equipment such as copiers, printers and computers. Big businesses have to contend with sick building syndrome and find it difficult to manage because of large office spaces and large numbers of people. You do not have this problem because it is only you or a few others in a smaller space. Open a window. Turn on an exhaust fan. Definitely purchase some type of environmental air system. The best air filter units use mechanical filtration methods which means you need to change the filters on a regular basis, usually every three to six months. The best ones also remove both gases and particulate matter. Do not purchase ionizers or ozone filters, and avoid promotions that offer a maintenance free unit. They are scams. Also, do not rely on your hot air furnace or air conditioner filters. They are worthless for all but "golf ball" size dust particles.

FOLLOW UP

Develop a follow-up program for getting back in touch with your customers or prospects. This regular reminder will keep you in their thoughts and either get you more business directly from them or lead to a qualified referral. Remember, the lifeblood of most businesses is referrals. These are infinitely stronger than trying to cultivate a new customer who knows nothing about you. There are several excellent computer software programs available to help you track your customers and prospects.

KEEP YOUR OFFICE NEAT

Although we usually meet our prospects or customers away from our home office, we keep our home office neat for those few times when it must be used for a meeting. Do not be embarrassed by having a home office especially if it is neat and well- organized. Your clients will respect you more if you are creating excellent work or making a professional presentation from modest surroundings. Often they may want to give you more business just to help you out versus going to a larger business where they may not be as appreciated. This is the *big fish* in the *little pond* method. Use it to your advantage.

KEEP CLUTTER TO A MINIMUM

Just because it is your home does not mean that you can let things pile up. Follow the seven-day rule. If mail, memos, faxes or other communications are over seven days old, either file them or throw them away. Use as many manila folders as you like. Make one location for outgoing mail and keep it there. Store important papers in a fireproof container. And above all, keep the kitty litter box away from your work area.

You will also need office equipment to save on home office expenses.

COPY MACHINES

It is almost impossible to get along without a copy machine. You can purchase a combination copier, fax machine and computer printer. The prices vary based on their capabilities. You can collate, staple, enlarge, reduce and copy on both sides. You can get black and white or color equipment. The higher the price, the more the features and the more it will cost you to service the machine. Also, the more the features, the greater the chance that your machine will rapidly be replaced with improved technology and lose value more quickly.

We experienced purchasing a machine through a lease/purchase program where we paid so much per month with an option to buy the machine at the lease termination. The payments looked good and the machine had all the features we needed except for stapling and two-sided copying. Two years after we leased it, our needs changed. We learned that we could have copies made for less money including the paper at an outside quick copy center. Our machine usage dropped to one or two copies at a time. When we attempted to sell it, we found out that it had the value of a boat anchor. What a rude awakening! It was as if we had thrown away $5,000. Unless you are flush with money and want to personally control everything you copy, purchase a machine that makes copies and only copies. You will be happy, and the machine will not depreciate as fast. The copies will look good and with the money left over, you can buy something else that you will need like a computer.

COMPUTERS

First, let it be known that we are computer dummies. There is an "on" switch and an "off" switch. If neither works, we are in trouble. Your type of business will play a major part in deciding what you need in a computer. However, the real determination of what computer you should purchase will be made by the types of software programs you will be running. Today's personal computer world is being driven by software. Bill Gates saw this first and built Microsoft into a dominating influence on the computer industry.

Software requires computer memory and speed which determine basic computer components. We are not going to recommend any particular type of computer, nor are we going to recommend any particular computer specifications. Even if we did, it would take less than six months for us to be out of date. What we will share with you is to get a computer and get it now. Do not delay. The knowledge you will gain today from using a computer that is obsolete in a couple years will outweigh any gain you may have had by waiting for the right time. There is no right time or right computer. Technology is moving too fast.

As far as we can tell, no business no matter how simple will be able to function *without* a computer. If you are computer dysfunctional, you are not alone. The majority of the population has yet to catch on. The best part is that while the computer is growing in its sophistication so, too, are the teaching aids to help you learn how to use them. More and more computer training schools are offering short courses on every software program. Sometimes, you can go to free courses offered by local business groups.

Many computer experienced people are now offering their services as "Software Coaches." These people come to your office and teach you how to use your computer and your software. Videotapes and books are coming out in record numbers. If you want help, it is there. The Internet has a multitude of web sites that share ideas and offer assistance. Technology advances in microchip production are resulting in more powerful computers at lower costs, further driving more and more people to start using them. With more users computers will become less costly and there will be more available support.

Soon it will not matter so much which particular computer or software package you have because of the Internet. New technology will allow us to have a "virtual office" on the Worldwide Web. The only equipment requirement may be a keyboard, a printer and a phone line, and for many the new satellite technology will eliminate the need for phone lines. This virtual office will allow us to access all our favorite software and provide unlimited storage for our files, eliminating the need for computer hardware. Imagine the ability to travel freely around the world without the need to carry a computer, backup files and program storage disks. In addition, think about the advantage of not having to worry about a hard disk failure and the related need for complicated backup files.

But, do not wait for this new technology. Get started today by adding a computer to your office. Do not worry about keeping up. We purchased what we thought was a great personal computer, but by the time it was one-year-old technology advances were already making it obsolete. In spite of this, we used that machine for over six years to adequately handle our needs. In those six years our skills grew. When it came time to get a new computer, we knew what we needed. Do not overspend. Stay with a basic computer and let your system needs evolve with your income-producing needs.

A true *Income Surfer* must have a computer to grow. It will help avoid or reduce many expenditures that might otherwise be necessary without it such as additional employees, accounting and office support services.

FAX MACHINES

Fax machines are indispensable! Whether you have a computer with a fax board or a stand-alone machine, you must have one. The ability to receive and transmit documents from a handwritten letter to a formal proposal is now a permanent part of business.

A separate fax in combination with a computer fax gives you another major advantage. You can use it as a scanner, if it has this capability. We regularly send documents from the fax machine to the computer. We then incorporate the document or graphic into another document. One type of software, called Optical Character Recognition (OCR), will also help eliminate a lot of retyping by allowing you to scan a written page directly into a word-processing program where it can be edited.

We have found that having both a computer fax and a stand-alone fax are necessary in our office. You will have to determine your needs and make that decision for yourself. If you get a stand-alone fax, make sure it has internal memory for at least twenty pages. This will automatically allow you to receive pages even when you run out of paper and to send broadcast faxes from memory.

TELECOMMUNICATIONS/PHONE SYSTEM

Your phone system may be very complex or very simple. If you are serious about your home business, you will need to have at least two (2) lines dedicated to it. One line is to receive all incoming calls and is the number you publicize. The second number is for outgoing calls and

is a "private" number not to be given out. Do not attempt to work your business with the same line as your home phone unless you are living alone and expect to receive only business calls.

Add *caller ID* to your line or lines. When you are on your outgoing line, you can monitor incoming calls for importance and decide whether to answer or to let your voice mail system handle it.

Telephone devices can now be purchased at a reasonable cost that can handle two lines, answer each line with the same or different incoming message, record the caller's message, include a speakerphone, allow for conferencing of the lines, and offer memory speed dial. We strongly recommend that you get a phone which has speakerphone capability. There may be many times when you want to listen to calls without having to hold the receiver in your hands, or you may want others in your office to listen along with you during a conference call or a phone presentation.

Another useful device is a portable phone headset that can be worn on your head. It has a high quality microphone and frees your hands for other work as well as saving your arms and ears from fatigue.

Many phone companies offer a variety of services such as *3-way calling*, *call waiting*, and *remote message answering*. Definitely get 3-way calling; it is growing in value as a business building tool. It will increase your credibility with your prospect or customer because you can connect an expert or someone else to answer their questions.

Toll-free numbers are no more costly than regular long-distance calls. A toll-free number gives more credibility and result in more business. Be careful about giving your toll-free number to everyone you meet unless you want a very large telephone bill at the end of the month. We reserve our toll-free numbers for moneymaking uses only. If someone abuses it we politely ask him or her to call us on our regular number.

Long-distance telephone companies are in fierce competition with each other, and you are their target. Prices on long-distance services are very competitive, and there may eventually be no difference between one company and another. The big differences will be in communications packages called *bundled* services. Some companies may offer you a special discounted rate if you buy other services from them. The number of services within a bundle will be determined by the telephone company and will be based on the competition. It definitely pays to shop around. You could save big sums of money.

When considering bundled packages, do not sign up for services you do not really need. The telephone company will be making money whether you use them or not through a basic monthly charge. Look at your needs. If your primary concern is long-distance calling, negotiate the best long-distance rate and look for the other services elsewhere.

A rapidly growing trend for long-distance services is to use a *debit calling card* which allows you to prepay for long-distance minutes at a greatly reduced rate. This is the fastest growing segment of telecommunications worldwide. When the minutes are used up, you either throw the card away or recharge it with more time. The best part is that no matter where you are--at home, in your office, in your car, on the road traveling--you can make calls at the same low rate. Telephone debit cards differ from telephone credit cards. Telephone credit cards are issued by a long-distance company who may not offer you a lower rate. Many of these cards carry a surcharge ("bong charge") for each call you make. These surcharges can add up. Debit cards have no per call surcharge.

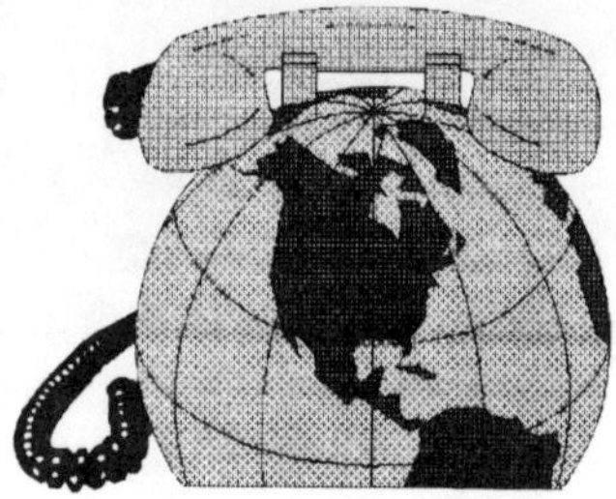

Cellular Phones and *Pagers* are now providing a big benefit to people--responsiveness. Having the ability to communicate any time and any place, can be very important depending on the type of business. Even if your business does not rest on critical communications, it is becoming more and more important to be responsive in a timely manner. It also costs you less money compared to paying for returned calls or, even worse, missing important calls.

We use both a pager and a cellular phone. Rather than give our cellular number to everyone, we give our pager number. This method allows us to screen the calls and to choose the time and method for responding to them. If you give out only your cellular number, you will be getting calls from everyone and paying for each one. With a pager you can select the calls to return and select the most economical way to call. Remember, you are charged for each cellular minute at a rate over and above your regular telephone charges.

Be careful about the type of cellular rate program you pick. The phone company will always win. You choose a higher monthly charge with a lower per minute charge including some "free" minutes or a lower monthly charge with a higher per minute rate. Either way you pay.

Practice call discipline with your cellular phone. All those little calls add up to a lot of minutes. A good rule is to ask yourself this question before each use of your cellular phone: "Is this call going to make me any money?" If the answer is no, look for a pay phone or make your call from a less costly source; perhaps you can wait until you are back at your office.

Cellular phone devices are allowing for more and more services to be connected to them as technology advances. Many people receive and send faxes from their cellular phones. People in retail can clear credit cards and checks from their portable phones. In the future, telecommunications will become much simpler as technology offers one number calling that will tie all your phones together. Cellular may remain an important part of this package, or it may be replaced with digital satellite systems. Regardless, if you are serious about being an independent businessperson and if you want to foster a professional image, you need to embrace cellular today and grow into these new programs as they evolve.

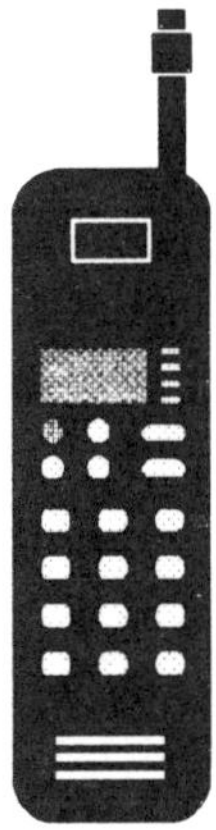

One final word about the Internet. New technology is making it possible to communicate voice, data, and video on the Internet at the same time. This merger of technologies is leading to a whole new competition among some very big telecommunications companies that could become a fierce war for customers. A few people are already making phone calls on the Internet for free. If the technology can be made reliable and the equipment mass marketed, we may be seeing another revolution that will forever reshape the telecommunications industry and how we communicate with each other. The independent business person working from home will have tremendous power right at his or her fingertips. What an opportunity!

Rule No. 1:
Never lose money.

Rule No. 2:
Never forget Rule No. 1.

--Warren Buffett[14]

[14] Warren Buffet is founder and Chairman of Berkshire Hathaway Industries a major stock investment and holding company.

Chapter 6

SUCCESS QUOTIENT (SQ) TESTING

I have a sixth sense, but not the other five. If I wasn't making money, they'd put me away.

--Red Skelton

Everyone has the ability to be successful in anything you attempt, if you believe you can. When it comes to business or being independent, many people lose confidence in their abilities because they have seen *other* people fail. This lack of confidence is not based on intelligence but on attitude.

Many modern-day success stories have come from people who did not give up or stop when they heard the word "No." Often these same people were also newcomers to the industries that they would eventually revolutionize. For example, look at Art Williams. He was a high school football coach who recognized that change needed to be made within the life insurance industry. His company, A. L. Williams Insurance, turned the insurance industry upside down and became part of the company that purchased one of the industry's oldest and strongest companies--The Travelers Insurance Company. Who could have predicted this? Then there is John Peterman who started with no experience or knowledge in mail-order and clothing apparel. He now operates one of the biggest mail-order clothing catalog businesses in the world--the J. Peterman Company. In debt without any experience and turned down by over 100 people when seeking capital, he still managed to win support from one major investor who recognized his vision and that he had a strong success attitude.

Another example is Fred Smith of Federal Express. Who could have predicted that a college student's simple idea to send letters and packages overnight would revolutionize the entire mail and shipping business? Today, the U.S. Postal Service, UPS and countless other overnight services owe a major part of their growth to the awareness that Fred Smith created in consumers' minds with his idea. Of course, mention has to be made about Microsoft's Bill Gates. He changed the world with the creation of DOS software and his vision that a box of electronic parts known as the computer could be turned into a tool that everyone could use. Just think about how the use of computers has accelerated progress in all walks of life. It is difficult to think of one area in which the computer has not made an impact. The ripple effect has been extraordinary!

When they started none of these people were guaranteed success. They just refused to accept failure. Yet in spite of their extraordinary successes, their capacity for success was no greater than the one each and everyone of us have within us. The ability to succeed in any venture is part of us all. No one is without it, unless we choose not to succeed.

One tool that measures success is a test. For a moment think about any formal test you have ever taken. Testing is part of our life from very early childhood through our formal education to employment opportunities and beyond. It is a way of measuring our past knowledge as well as our capacity to learn. We are constantly being tested. But, how do we test for success? In other words, how do we measure our *capacity* for success? This is very difficult. If such a test existed and if it could be objectively scored, it would revolutionize everything from running for political office to starting a new business to inventing a new product--virtually anything requiring definiteness of purpose, vision and focus.

That is the unusual thing about the capacity for success. It is difficult to measure or predict because it can happen to anyone at any time when the right elements come together. Finding a test that could apply to everyone for every situation is not practical; however, there is a test that has merit and may provide some key direction for someone who takes it. This test checks your "Success Quotient (SQ)."[15] Like "Intelligence Quotient (IQ)," which measures capacity for learning, there is the way to measure capacity for success. Having a high IQ does not demonstrate success nor does it guarantee it. But, if you knew you had a high IQ, you might have a stronger belief in your ability to learn. Similarly, if you know you have a high SQ, you might also have a stronger belief in your ability to succeed.

Income Surfing increases a person's odds for success by spreading the ability to earn money across a broader base of income sources. It is simply a function of strength in numbers. The results of the SQ test can reinforce one's capacity to become a successful *Income Surfer*.

---

[15] *Success Quotient Test* used with permission. Copyright 1995 **Success Networks International**—publishing SUCCESS STRATEGIES, SUCCESS DIGEST, and INSIGHT. Success Net is dedicated to helping its members become more knowledgeable, prosperous and effective. For a free subscription to SUCCESS DIGEST, mailto:majordomo@webcoach.com with SUBSCRIBE SDIGEST-LIST in the body of the message. Free trial membership at http://www.successnet.org mailto:success@successnet.org

Take the following test with an open-mind regardless of your experience or education. Relax and have fun. Part of becoming successful in anything is to have a good sense of humor, a realistic viewpoint of your capabilities and the willingness to turn weakness into strength.

Here is the "***Success Quotient Test***"

Directions: Answer the following questions. Put your score in the blank. When you have finished, add up your scores and rate yourself. Where applicable, 10 is the highest.

1. You read at least _____ personal growth books a year. (Give yourself 2 points for each.) ___
2. You speak well in front of small groups. (scale of 1-10) ___
3. You have a good exercise program: i.e., 30 minutes a day, 3 times per week. (scale 1-10) ___
4. You have written and specific goals. (10 Yes, 0 No) ___
5. You have an excellent vocabulary and challenge yourself to continue vocabulary building. (scale 1-10) ___
6. You have set goals in each of the following six areas: 1. Financial and Career 2. Physical and Health 3. Family 4. Social and Cultural 5. Educational 6. Spiritual. (Give yourself 5 points for each area and an extra 10 points if you have goals in *all* areas.) ___
7. You keep commitments--to yourself as well as others. (scale of 1-10) ___
8. You can clearly articulate your three most important goals. (10 Yes, 0 No) ___

9. You have a plan of action to achieve financial independence. (scale of 1-10) ___
10. You have an excellent relationship with your family. (scale of 1-10) ___
11. You smoke. (minus 5 Yes, 5 No) ___
12. Alcohol use. (5 abstain; 2 moderate; minus 5, drink excessively) ___
13. You have a written personal mission statement (10 Yes, 2 if you know what one is, 0 if no clue) ___
14. Your weight. (minus 5 if more than 20 pounds overweight) ___
15. You have a positive mental attitude. (scale of 1-10) ___
16. You have a fulfilling occupation. (scale of 1-10) ___
17. You have a healthy balance between leisure and work. (scale 1-10) ___

TOTAL POINTS _____

YOUR RATING: If you scored -

150 points or higher, you are a Super Success: You are constantly achieving your goals and setting new ones. A definite winner!

100 points or higher, you are a High Achiever: You can expect to reach most of your goals and you have good balance in your life.

75 points or higher, you are a Success: You are on the road to success--therefore you are a success.

20 points or more, you are a Survivor: You probably will not set any records (unless you change your ways), but you will get by.

Less than 20 Points, you are a Loser: There are none. They do not take these kinds of tests nor would they read this publication.

Check your score against the ratings listed above.

Where do you stand? Understand that this test is only a measurement of where you are today. Unlike physical limitations that may not allow for someone to overcome them, limitations associated with success are primarily from weaknesses in attitude. Attitudes can be changed. They can be replaced or strengthened. Eighty percent of success in today's life is based on attitude. Only 20 percent is based on what we know (knowledge).

If you scored low on the SQ Test, make a pact with yourself to start changing your attitude today. Identify your weaknesses and focus on your strengths.

If you scored high on the SQ Test, make a pact with yourself to stop wasting time in moving toward your success goals. Time is a precious asset that cannot be replaced.

Understanding yourself is a major key to finding the right formula leading to your success. The SQ Test has already given you some valuable personal insight, but it is important for you to have as much understanding of yourself as possible. So, here's another self-evaluation called *"Do You Have What It Takes?"*[16]

Directions: Write yes or no in the blank provided at the end of each question or statement below.

1. Do I have a close relative in business for himself/herself? ___
2. Did I ever work for a small firm where I had close contact with the person who started it? ___

---

[16] Sources for *"Do You Have What It Takes?"*- Jeffrey Sushauer and the Entrepreneur Institute, Worthington, Ohio; Sara Shifrin, Chicago-based consultant.

3. Did I ever work for a small division of a larger firm where I had close contact with the top manager? ____
4. Is my work experience in a variety of functional areas, such as marketing, finance and production? ____
5. Has my employer ever rejected my "better mousetrap" idea? ____
6. I can make up my mind in a hurry if I have to. It usually turns out OK, too. ____
7. I have lived in three or more cities. ____
8. I have been fired. ____
9. My spouse is supportive of my work (if married). ____
10. What generally happens to me is something I make happen, not something that is due to luck, good or otherwise. ____
11. If I had to choose between working for a firm I do not own for twice the money I make now, and running my own firm at present pay, I would choose my own firm. ____
12. When a problem comes up that everyone says is unsolvable, I usually try to figure out ways to solve it. ____
13. As a child, I sold lemonade or had a paper route or similar activities. ____
14. I get along with other people. ____
15. My subordinates respect and work hard for me, even if they do not necessarily like me. ____
16. I like to have a plan before I start. I'm usually the one to get things lined up when the group wants to do something. ____

TOTAL YES SCORE ____

Scoring Key: If you answered yes 13 to 16 times, get started on your business plan; 10 to 12 times, you have potential, but need to push yourself a little; 6 to 9 times, you can do it, but have a way to go; 0 to 5 times, maybe self-employment is not for you.

He who asks of life nothing but the improvement of his own nature...is less liable than anyone else to miss and waste life.

- Henri Frederic Amiel[17]

[17] Henri Frederic Amiel noted Swiss critic (1821-1881)

Chapter 7

THE SMALL OFFICE/HOME OFFICE (SOHO) & HOME BASED BUSINESSES

> **Professionals are people who can do their job when they don't feel like it. Amateurs are people who can't do their job when they do feel like it.**
>
> --Anonymous

Go to any newsstand and look at the business section. You will find a growing list of publications that emphasize some type of small office, home office, or home based business. The acronym assigned to this group is SOHO. The people working from a SOHO involve a wide diversity of occupations and industries. This rapidly growing group is becoming a significant force within the North American economy as well as around the world.

The major difference between a small office and the home office is its location. A small office is located away from the home in a separate structure. This could be a shared office complex or a stand-alone building. Often a small office is located in a former residential home that has been converted into a commercial building. One major selection reason for operating out of a small office versus the home office is usually image or appearance. A small office occupant may have a stronger need for bringing customers or prospects to the office. For example, a medical services or equipment distributor may want an office where a small display can be set up to view products. Another reason may be for presentations or meetings with clients. Or, in other cases the small office occupant represents a much larger company that wants to maintain a separate office for image purposes. In many cases the need for other office support services may dictate the decision. On the other hand, there are many home offices which in terms of decor and location are formidable rivals to a small office. As a matter of fact, a goodly number of people find their home offices to be much more comfortable for meeting with both customers and prospects. The bottom line is basically one of personal preference.

A major part of the SOHO growth is the trend toward the home based businesses. So important is this trend that it needs to be addressed in additional detail. This trend toward home based businesses is being called by some the "Quiet Revolution"-- the movement of over 8,000 people per day starting a home business. That is one home based business every 11 seconds![18] Here are some facts driving this movement.

- Ninety-five percent of home based businesses survive their first year compared to only 50 percent for traditional business start-ups.

[18] *Home Business News Report* printed by Freecom Communications 1994.

- Over a three-year period 85 percent of home based businesses survive compared with only 25 percent for traditional businesses. [19]

A New York City-based business research firm reports that the average home based business household earns $50,250 a year.[20] This is almost double the $26,000 annual salary the average U.S. employee makes. About 20 percent of all home business households earn in excess of $75,000 a year and it is not uncommon for home-based franchisees to generate over $100,000 annually in profits.[21] No wonder this trend is rapidly growing!

Do you realize that big business, the Fortune 500 companies, account for a negative employment growth, but that over the decades of the 1980s and 1990s small businesses accounted for all positive job growth in the U.S?[22] According to the *American Home Business Association* a total of 1,500 jobs are lost every day in the U.S. and Fortune 500 companies have eliminated over 5 million jobs in the past decade. The growth is in businesses with less than 20 employees.

Further backing up this powerful movement are the actual figures stated in *The New York Times 1998 Almanac.*

> Small businesses account for 99 percent of the 23.3 million non-farm businesses in the United States today, according to the Small Business

[19] Research provided by Link Resources, New York, NY.
[20] Ibid
[21] *Home Business* Magazine, Feb. 1998, Article by Marcus P. Meleton, Jr. titled "Franchises Can Light Your Fire" page 94.
[22] Statistics taken from *The New York Times 1998* Almanac pages 352-364

> Administration. Sole proprietorships make up 16.7 million of these small businesses, while 1.6 million are partnerships, and 5 million are corporations (these figures are based on tax returns, so the number of sole proprietorships may be inflated by artists, freelance writers, and other self-employed people who are not technically [considered] businesses). As of 1996, small businesses employ 53 percent of the private work force, make 47 percent of all sales in America, and account for 51 percent of all private sector output. According to the Department of Labor, about 750,000 new small businesses are created every year; about 10 percent of them fail. [23]

Bill Gates, the founder and president of Microsoft Corporation as well as the second richest man in the world, recently stated that he does not fear competition from big business but fears it from the small start-up business being built in somebody's garage or basement. In fact he should know--Microsoft started this way.[24]

In a recent issue of the *USA Today* [25]newspaper, it was reported that nearly 65% of all Americans own or say they have dreamed of starting a small business.

The following figure lists the things they said were their major concerns:

---

[23] *The New York Times 1998 Almanac* page 364

[24] Presentation before the United States Congress March 3, 1998

[25] *USA Today* March 1996 front page. Research by Roper Starch Worldwide Survey for Quickbooks from Intuit.

Figure 5. Most Important to Start Business

Time to Devote to It	**91%**
Start-up Money	**87%**
Marketable Idea	**84%**
Business, Finance Skills	**74%**

Knowing all of this, it certainly becomes clear why aware people are searching for ways to build an independent income from their homes or a small office. In addition, with the increasing numbers of new people starting some type of small business, the stage has been set for new ideas and business directions which will definitely shape their future. After all, almost every big business we know today had to start with an idea and with somebody convinced enough to prove it would work.

In September 1997, slightly more than 7.8 million workers, representing 6 percent of the work force, had two jobs, according to the Bureau of Labor Statistics. And, the percentage of employees with two jobs rose from 5.9% in 1994 to 6.2 percent in 1996. Of the nearly 8 million people holding two jobs, 238,000 work full time at both positions.[26]

According to the trend above, smart people are realizing that the only way to secure the future is to start second, third and fourth jobs--although the word *job* is more and more starting to mean some type of *independent* income. This trend is one of the primary driving forces behind the explosion in small business. Regardless of the location--

[26] Article by Steven Ginsberg, *Washington Post* newspaper, printed in *Hartford Courant* March 9, 1998 page D7.

small office or home office--it is very clear the movement is here to stay and will be a growing force in tomorrow's world.

In later chapters we will discuss in more detail the opportunities of the SOHO, and we will take a closer look at how to keep more of the money you earn. Again, the rule for operating on your own is simple—*It's Not What You Earn It's What You Keep!*

A man with a surplus can control circumstances, but a man without a surplus is controlled by them, and often he has no opportunity to exercise judgment.

--Harvey S. Firestone[27]

[27] Harry S. Firestone (1868-1938), founder Firestone Tire & Rubber Company

Chapter 8

TAKING CONTROL OF YOUR LIFE

If someone is going down the wrong road, he doesn't need motivation to speed him up. What he needs is education to turn him around.

--Jim Rohn[28]

Are you at the end of your rope? Have you tried things that just did not work out? Are you frustrated with where you are and with what you are doing? Are you *sick and tired of being sick and tired?*

We know you are reading this book to better your life financially. We also know you are looking for the "How To's" of *Income Surfing*. Just knowing this information is not enough. You must understand what is happening in the world around you, too.

[28] Jim Rohn is recognized as America's foremost business philosopher.

Therefore, we assume that you are reading this book because you want to grow as a person in addition to maturing financially and materially.

Reading books and listening to tapes is one way to grow personally. At the end of this book is a recommended list of books and tapes that will help you. You may have read books and listened to tapes that have had a particular impact on your life which are not on the list. If so, please tell us about them. We are reading and listening to new ones all the time. It is important that you have a regular self-help program that you follow. The human mind is both wondrous and underused. It can absorb information it is exposed to even in the subconscious. And, the subconscious mind can recall information and use it to drive the conscious mind in a particular direction.

A good example of this is using pictures to reinforce a goal or desire. Let is say you would like to own a particular type of house or car. Find a picture of what you want that is as close as possible to what you desire. Make copies of the picture. (If it is a color picture make color copies.) Hang the pictures in prominent locations around your home, office and automobile, and keep a picture in your wallet or purse. Every time you are in front of the picture think about achieving your goal. Over time, without consciously realizing it, your subconscious mind will be directing your conscious mind to actions that will lead to what you have pictured. It may not happen overnight, but it *will* happen.

Another positive reinforcement is to carry with you a list of written goals that you can look at on a regular basis. The continuous reinforcement will also remind your subconscious of what you desire and that you are serious about reaching the goal. Again, it may not happen quickly, and it may not be exactly what you wrote down, but it will be close enough. *Without* this positive reinforcement your chances of reaching your goals are dramatically reduced.

Taking control of your life means doing those things that keep you on track. It will not be easy because the world is basically negative and its forces will work to push you off course. Just like sailing a boat or flying an airplane, you must constantly look at your compass and make minor corrections to your course. Going from point to point and making a series of small corrections are much easier than going far off course and having to make a large correction. Sometimes large corrections are just not possible and we end up hopelessly lost. In a sailboat or airplane this is bad enough, but if we let our life go hopelessly off course, it could be a miserable disaster and hurt others around us in the process.

When getting started in *Income Surfing*, you are making a conscious decision to take control of your life. One goal of *Income Surfing* is to regain financial control. To do this will require your full attention. It will be the little things that you do every day which will add up to reaching your goal. Like the minor course corrections previously mentioned, you will do something each day to advance yourself. *Income Surfing* will not happen immediately, but it will happen. As you gain control over one income source and learn to manage it properly, you will gain the freedom to look for other interesting income sources which can be added. Doing so will increase your productivity and financial rewards.

There is no better feeling than waking up in the morning knowing that you are the master of your own destiny. And, this means more than financial destiny. If you can wake up to a day where you can set your own schedule, make your own decisions, exercise your imagination, be creative in your thinking, and make an idea come to life, you are in control. *Income Surfing* can do this for you.

If there was ever a reason to take control of your life, it is the times we are living in today. In the book titled *The Great Reckoning,* the authors, James Dale Davidson and Lord William Rees-Moog, detailed their findings from an in-depth study of modern man's economic and political history. History does indeed repeat itself, and we must learn from our past mistakes to avoid problems in the future. [29]

To understand why you must take control of your life now, you must understand what is happening in the world.

The three revolutions of human life, the tribalization of society, and the decline of America are some compelling historical facts with a modern perspective detailed in *The Great Reckoning.* This information helps explain why you *need* to take responsibility for your life today through *Income Surfing*.

> **The median net financial assets of Americans earning from $40,000-$50,000 a year, including cash, savings accounts and bond are $1,200.**
>
> --Roger Porter[30]

---

[29] *The Great Reckoning* by James Dale Davidson and Lord William Rees-Moog. Published by Simon & Schuster, 1993, New York, NY.
[30] Roger Porter, White House Advisor on Domestic Policy, 1989

Figure 6. Compelling Historical Facts

The Three Revolutions of Human Life

6,000 B.C. - Agricultural

People went from nomads and foragers to staying in one place.

1490s - Gunpowder

The balance of power was changed and put in the hands of more people

1990s - Information

Information may be manipulated on smaller scale and power is shifting to small groups and even individuals. The power brokers of the future will control the *microchip*.

The Tribalization of Society

- Military power of small groups is increasing.
- Power is devolving.
- Violence in society is on the increase.
- Government is becoming hard-pressed to stop violence.
- Economic decline and electronic feudalism may result.
- Breakdown of public order will expose people to dangers of predatory violence.
- Vigilantism is increasing to protect lives and property.
- As the costs of urban life and misgovernment increase, those who can afford to will retreat from the cities to the countryside.

The Decline of America

- America is following in Britain's footsteps.
- Intellectuals are rejecting the American way of life and capitalism in general.
- More groups are raising claims of "oppression."

- Racism is increasing whereby people judge others according to race, sex, religion or some other characteristic.
- The national debt grows as federal spending grows.
- By mid-1980s the national debt for one year exceeded the gross national product of 158 of 167 countries. Debt interest payments in America alone are greater than all individual taxable income tax collected from everyone West of the Mississippi River.
- Politicians fail to make tough choices and become less responsive and more entrenched the longer they are in office.
- Productivity is slipping while Japan's is increasing three times and European productivity is growing at two times the U.S. rate.
- The U.S. has ceased to be internationally competitive. Exports look like those of an underdeveloped country. The top six are corn seed, soybeans, coal, wood, cotton, and wheat.
- Top U.S. imports from Japan are automobiles, tape recorders, trucks, office machines, parts for office machines and computer chips.
- The U.S. has become "a natural resource colony" for Japan.
- America's education system is more adept at training people to redistribute wealth rather than to create it.
- Ten lawyers graduate for every engineer, as compared to ten engineers for every lawyer in Japan.
- In 1990 there were more lawyers in the U.S. than in the rest of world.
- The U.S. has four times more lawyers per capita than Great Britain, five times more than Germany, ten times more than France, and twenty times more than Japan.
- There are 50,000 lawyers in Washington, D.C.--more than in all of Japan.

- The cost for lawsuits in the U.S. is 400 times higher than in other advanced economies.
- The legal system does more harm than good. It promotes crime.
  - Odds are 100:1 to escape punishment for a crime in the U.S.
  - Crime rate in the U.S. is 1700% higher than in Japan.
- Between 1975 and 1988 over one million security guards were hired because they are less costly to train and more efficient to deploy than regular law enforcement personnel. The average policeman costs over $150,000 to put on the street but only spends 2 percent of the time patrolling. Most of his or her time is spent responding to crises.
- For every $100 spent on law enforcement, only $2 to $3 is spent to prevent crime.
- Billions are spent on locks and security devices without results.
- *Health Care* expense is both a cause and a consequence of America growing poorer.
  - Rapid cost escalation in noncompetitive health services disguises a weaker economy while making it poorer.
  - From March 1991 to October 1992 health care jobs rose by 430,000 while all other employment rose 65,000. (In other words had health care not expanded, the net U.S. employment would have fallen by 365,000 jobs in that period.)
  - It looks like the growth of the U.S. economy is tied to the health care system. (We can all get rich by getting sick and paying each other ever more inflated sums for health care programs.)
  - Americans appeared to get richer because they paid for health care that people in other developed nations bought for less.

- For Dr. Henry Heimlich who invented the Heimlich Maneuver, his cancer therapy in the U.S. costs $300,000 a week. In Mexico it would cost $15,000 a week, and in China $2,000 a week, using the same therapy and same technology!
- The explosion in costs has not significantly bettered statistical measures of health. Greek men live longer than Americans with one-tenth the outlay for medical care.

◆At the present rate, American health care costs will absorb the entire U.S. economy in the next century. (Bankruptcy will occur first!)

- In 1980, 9 percent of disposable income went to health care; in 1992 it jumped to 14.6 percent.
- Individual bankruptcies due to health care lead to calls for a national health care system. People who go broke have to ask someone else to pay the bills. This is a marker on the road to national bankruptcy.

◆The U.S. has ceased to act like a creditor. It acts like a debtor.

The results of the decline of America are many.

◆Reliance on foreign capital is unsustainable in the long run.

◆The dollar's value will fall and further reduce American living standards.

◆Minority interest groups will raise concerns about uncontrolled entreprenuerism and free enterprise.

◆State control will increase. [31]

History helps us to understand what we need to do for the future. Historical statistics provide an insight about current trends and how they may relate to the future. Whether you

---

[31] Historical facts excerpted from *The Great Reckoning* by James Dale Davidson and Lord William Rees-Moog. Published by Simon & Schuster, 1993, New York, NY.

agree with the findings detailed above or not is up to you. But, we must not ignore the signals coming from the world around us. We are extremely optimistic about the future and the economic opportunities that are and will be available. We are also optimistic about the U.S. political system and the ability of this country's citizens to make decisions and changes when they are in everyone's best interest. No other country offers the same potential for advancement or lifestyle.

However, like all political economic systems, it is only as good as the people it is designed to protect, and it is the duty of these people to take as much responsibility for themselves as possible without relying on the government to do so. Some politicians would have us believe that people are incapable of taking care of themselves and that government *must* fill this role through regulations and increased funding for government support programs. If you listen to supporters of these programs long enough, you will begin to think they are right. For example, suppose one morning you wake up feeling perfectly fine and healthy. The first person you see at work asks you, "*Do you feel all right?*" The second person you meet says, "*You look a little pale. Do you have temperature?*" And, the third person you meet observes, "*You don't sound so good.*" By now you may think they are right and answer, "*You know, I am feeling a little down. Perhaps I should go home to rest!*"

Therefore we recommend that people do the following.

- Start taking responsibility for their own futures.
- Harness technologies and information systems.
- Work from the home.
- Develop multiple source income bases through *Income Surfing*.

- Build national and international income bases.
- Stop voting for new social programs.
- Change lifestyles to prevent disease and sickness.
- Start building wealth instead of depleting it.
- Be creative and constructive in your actions to become a "giver" versus a "taker."

Laughter is the best medicine and keeps life from getting too serious on us. Figure 7 provides a different viewpoint of the time dedicated to work.

Figure 7. So You Want a Day Off?!

Let's take a moment to look at what you are asking for.
There are 365 days available for work.
There are 52 weeks per year, of which you already have 2 days off each weekend, leaving 262 days left for work.
Since you spend 16 hours each day away from work, that accounts for 170 days.
There are 91 days available for work.
You spend 30 minutes each day on breaks, that accounts for 23 days each year, leaving 68 days available for work.
You spend one hour a day for lunch, that accounts for another 46 days per year, leaving 22 days available for work.
You spend 2 days per year on sick leave, leaving 20 days available for work.
You take 9 holidays per year, leaving 11 days available for work.
You take 10 days vacation each year, leaving 1 day left available for work.
No way are you going to take that day off.

Source Unknown

Chapter 9

How To *Income Surf*

It is our philosophical set of the sail that determines the course of our lives. To change our current direction, we have to change our philosophy not our circumstances.

--Jim Rohn[32]

You are doing well! You have made it this far which means you are motivated. Many people give up early when faced with learning something new, especially if it requires a little work.

Once you understand the *Income Surfing* philosophy, the next step is to learn how to do it. Like learning how to ride a bike, roller-skate, or fly an airplane, *Income Surfing* also requires that it be done in progressive steps. Since you may start to learn *Income Surfing* while you have a full-time job or business, it would be a major mistake to try to take on more than two income sources at first.

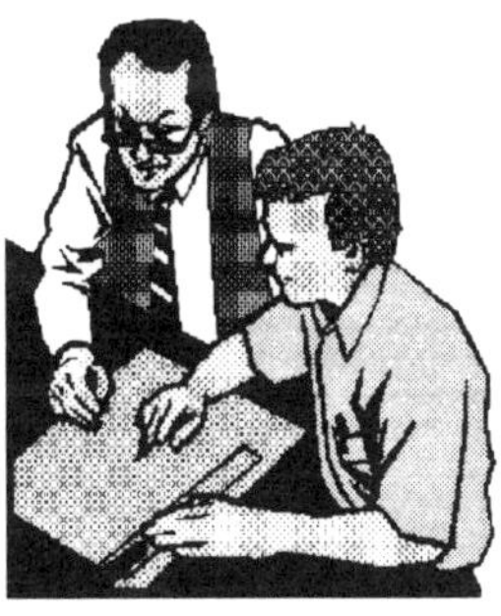

[32] Jim Rohn is recognized as America's foremost business philosopher

This holds true for everyone regardless of background. We have seen even the most sophisticated businessperson melt when taking on too much of something he or she did not understand.

As mentioned earlier, we started *Income Surfing* before we were aware of the term, *Income Surfing*. Like someone who falls off a cliff and lands in a river, if you want to survive, you either know how to swim or you learn very quickly. That is what happened to us. The only difference was that we had fallen into a financial river full of swift water and dangerous rapids. Our motivation to take on multiple sources of income was desperation. Jim Rohn has said "We generally change ourselves for one of two reasons: inspiration or desperation." That is where we were. One of us (Bob) was rapidly losing control over a growing aviation business because of a poor partner arrangement, and the other (Ken) was fighting financial ruin due to tax law changes responsible for collapsing an investment company he had helped build.

When you are young there is less of a financial sense of urgency in life. Trying times look temporary. There is a feeling of invincibility, even immortality. You think that whatever is lost can easily be regained. As you grow older the feeling of invincibility is replaced with your sense of mortality. The ability to replace financial losses takes on a more realistic and sobering appearance. We often urge younger people to get to work now while they have their youthful energy. Why wait until you are forty or fifty years old to learn what to do when you can start doing it now?

This is what is so exciting about *Income Surfing*. It can be done when you are young or old. It is just a matter of perspective and attitude.

Getting started is the most important step. Here are eight steps to take when starting to *Income Surf.*

1. Self-evaluate your strengths and weakness. Make a written list and be honest.
2. Make a list of your goals: short-term ones to accomplish in less than one year and long-term ones that will take two to five years.
3. List the real as well as the perceived obstacles to your goals.
4. Make a list of people or groups that can help you reach your goals.
5. List skills and learning requirements needed to reach your goals.
6. Write a plan of action.
7. List those tasks which you love to do, that make you happy when doing them and what you would do if money were not a problem.
8. List everything that you will gain by reaching your goals.

Completing the above steps will have immense value once you have made up your mind to get started in *Income Surfing,* a process that develops over time and is based in large part on your willingness to manage yourself and to stay organized.

Just about any previous experience can become an asset in *Income Surfing*. If you were conscientious in your education or experience, you are probably above average in your knowledge. There are many ways to apply this experience and knowledge for financial rewards.

At this point we will assume that you are not seeking a traditional job but want a situation that compensates you while leaving you free time for other tasks such as *Income Surfing*. Remember that your time is your most precious asset.

Your goal should be to use *Income Surfing* as a way to maintain your freedom from limited, low-paying and unrewarding careers.

Remember, the hardest door to go through is your own.

On the other side exists a whole new world of opportunity.

Chapter 10

SOME EXAMPLES OF *INCOME SURFING*

If you are not willing to risk the unusual,
you will have to settle for the ordinary.
--Jim Rohn

Intelligently applied, *Income Surfing* can work for almost anyone from any background.

Comfortability, compatibility and time are the keys to picking an income source for *Income Surfing*.

COMFORTABILITY

It is critical that you select a business that makes you comfortable and is fun to work. For *Income Surfing* to work, you must be able to turn things "on" and "off." It is easier to be flexible about something you like and find comfortable.

For example, you may love to play tennis. You may also be an experienced home improvement contractor who wants to diversify your income. Look for something that can marry these two experiences together such as resurfacing tennis courts or marketing tennis supplies to people who have their own private tennis courts. This way you can be around the tennis game while you work. You can elect to say something when you make a contact or you can make a note to call the person at a more appropriate time.

Suppose you recently retired from a job as store manager for a large retail store chain. You enjoy working with people and still feel young and have many good ideas. Why not use your experience to help new start-up stores or businesses get going? Local chambers of commerce have contacts throughout the community that could feed you situations requiring your knowledge. You could work when and where you choose. In addition, you will meet new people who could lead you to opportunities and other new alternative income sources. You would then be developing a consulting business. Many consultants have developed a multitude of clients in diverse areas. Again, spreading your income sources over a broad base is the goal.

COMPATIBILITY

This second key is very important. The things you choose to work at must be compatible or symbiotic with the other things you are doing. This means that if you are going in one direction, it is easy for you to carry your other things with you. It also means that when one thing is not working, you can bring in another as an alternative.

For example, suppose you have a sales position to market hydraulic valves to businesses. You must travel a specific territory that covers several states. You spend three days a week traveling and two days a week in a home office. While you travel from one account to another you pass many other businesses. Let us assume you have another source of income, selling environmental products. These products are excellent for small businesses such as lawyers, accountants, printshops, or any place where people spend a lot of time indoors.

In your travels from one hydraulic valve customer to another, you make it a point to stop at several of these other businesses on the way. Over time, you develop a customer following and between referrals and repeat business you have another income.

Another example is that you love to fly and are a pilot part-time. You also operate a small scrap metals business where you make pickups on an as needed basis. Your schedule allows you to decide when you make trips for business or pleasure. You decide to attend a national aviation convention. While you are there you will promote digital wristwatches you can purchase very inexpensively from the manufacturer because of production overruns. As you walk around the convention having fun meeting people and looking at the aviation exhibits, you promote the watches. You sell out and take everyone's phone number for follow-up. These customers become your business base for marketing other products as you add them.

TIME

The third key is to not allow any one thing to monopolize your time.

Remember, time is your greatest asset. People who give up control of their time also give up much of their freedom to keep moving ahead.

As mentioned above, one area that you can apply your knowledge and experience is in *consulting*. Consultant expertise is always useful. At any given time there is a market for their skills. In today's rapidly changing world, everyone is seeking new information on where they stand and where they must go. Small and large companies face this same challenge. Hiring a consultant to conduct market research or to evaluate a situation is becoming more common. Outside expertise or consulting has taken on an expanded role as business in general continues to streamline. Be open to opportunities that are time limited or, in other words, those things that will occupy you for a few months or even a few weeks. Some consultant situations are not based on time but on projects or programs where a task is completed for a fixed fee.

Writing business plans, marketing manuals and employee handbooks are some of the things that we have done as consultants. This required our experience and the ability to research those areas in which we had no knowledge. Our compensation was in large part based on how well we could organize ourselves to get the job done versus relying on experience alone. Many of you can do the same things even if you have modest experience. The ability to use a computer with its various word-processing and accounting programs will be of great help to you.

Whatever you decide to do, be sure that you respect your time. Use it to the fullest. For years we have told *people to work full-time in your part-time*. It is amazing how many people allow time to be wasted on nonproductive things.

We feel that the growth of people who engage in *Income Surfing* is unlimited. These people tell only a fraction of what is possible, but this will give you a place to begin your search.

We interviewed real *Income Surfers*. Some are just getting started while others are highly experienced at it. Their stories follow.

Bill Stanley lives in North Carolina and has been an avid *Income Surfer* for over twenty years. At one time, Bill owned a successful landscaping business but suffered from seasonal variations and the related unpredictable income. He began to sell real estate to enhance his income. Now he owns a restaurant and a video games business. He also manages land lease, sells telecommunications services, and markets pre-paid legal services.

Jay Ireland lives in Georgia outside Atlanta. At one time he was a dedicated corporate employee with what he thought was a secure future. When that abruptly ended, Jay took his knowledge and created his own mortgage broker business. He then added telecommunications and digital satellite direct sales. Now, he is also managing an investment portfolio created for himself and his wife. Jay strongly believes that *Income Surfing* is the future and is still looking for other income sources to add to it.

John Collins is President and CEO of Hartford Toner & Cartridge, Inc., a firm that specializes in service and supplies for office machines. John is known all over Connecticut for his energy, business success and promotional appearances dressed as his alter ego *TONERMAN©*—cape, leotard, shorts and all. John believes strongly in multiple source incomes. Besides running a very busy company and giving time to his growing family, he runs a second business called Auto-Connection that helps people shop for vehicles from home. He also owns and manages commercial and residential income properties in several states, and maintains an aggressive mutual fund investment program that he automatically contributes funds to monthly.

Mike Carlo is from Connecticut. He is married with two young children and has an office at home in addition to a regular office building office. Mike worked as a land surveyor and now has a land acquisition and development business that caters to builder's and individual owners. His success led him to become an investment account executive with a major brokerage firm. And, based on an interest he had in high school for marine biology, he is part of an aqua-culture partnership operating a growing clam farm business.

Steve Nephew lives in Florida and has been *Income Surfing* off and on for over 20 years. After a major health setback, Steve felt he needed to make multiple source incomes a full-time goal. He presently earns money as a teacher, financial/investment advisor. He also markets insurance and has a direct sales digital satellite TV business. He states that he needed to leverage his time for both income and schedule freedom, and it was the personal flexibility that made *Income Surfing* a key part of his life.

Nanette Miner lives in Connecticut. She is married and works with her husband's video production company as a project researcher and writer. She has had a home office for over seven years. Nanette has a background in training and development and writes management programs for manufacturing firms. She also does business coaching for entrepreneurs and new management personnel. She is an author with one published book marketed over the Internet and has two more books on the way. In addition, she operates a national direct sales business in the nutrition and health industry and most recently acquired a self-service dog washing salon business.

Chapter 11

LEARNING TO DREAM AGAIN

It is difficult to say what is impossible, for the dream of yesterday is the hope of today and the reality of tomorrow.

--Robert H. Goddard [33]

A big part of life is being able to dream. Children dream about everything: what they want to be when they grow up, where they want to live, who they want to marry, and what they want to do with their life. What a wonderful thing dreaming is!

Yet, in spite of the excitement and wonder children gain from dreaming, most of them grow up to be adults who stop dreaming. These people lose the skill to dream or perhaps even worse, somebody destroys their desire to dream. But, dreams create new life. Dreams create energy to accomplish. People who dream about what they want out of life and who strive to make their dreams come true are what make the world go around.

---

[33] Robert H. Goddard (1882-1945). American physicist and rocket pioneer. Graduate of Worcester Polytechnic Institute, Worcester, MA

Art Williams, the very successful founder of A. L. Williams Insurance, wrote about dreaming in his book, *All You Can Do*. His six steps to success are:

1. Become a dreamer again.
2. Have a crusade.
3. Dream big but keep it simple.
4. Always be positive.
5. Treat people good.
6. Never give up. [34]

What powerful advice! Art Williams created a revolution in the life insurance industry because he had a dream.

People stop dreaming because they allow their lives to be controlled by others. This has nothing to do with government or laws. It has everything to do with allowing oneself to become subservient to the will of others even if there is a better direction or way to do something that could benefit everyone. Failure to exercise one's own initiative and ideas acts to suppress imagination, a big part of dreaming. Over time both imagination and dreaming will atrophy and eventually disappear.

One major reason we find *Income Surfing* so vital to our lives is that it has allowed us to dream again. As related earlier, we have experienced losing everything and having to start all over again. It is at this point that it is the easiest to give up by allowing someone else to take over the responsibility for our life. But, we decided not to let that happen. In addition, we also decided that we had to avoid being put in danger of that ever happening in the future.

[34] *All You Can Do is All You Can Do* by A.L. Williams, published 1988 by Oliver-Nelson Books, Nashville, TN.

Through *Income Surfing*'s multiple income base, we were able to create a foundation to prevent failure.

Income Surfing creates a financial foundation that fosters dreams. Once established, *Income Surfing*'s multiple incomes remove the crippling effects of having one income source and of having to cater to it. By working at multiple incomes that you can control, yourself, the overall effect is to create security. This security replaces what was once the major attraction of a job with corporate America.

If one advances confidently in the directions of his dreams, and endeavors to live the life which he has imagined, he will meet with a success unexpected in common hours.

--Henry David Thoreau

Chapter 12

RESIDUAL INCOMES FOR *INCOME SURFERS*

We should not expect something for nothing but we all do, and we call it hope.
--Ed Howe[35]

Hope is a wonderful thing. Without hope life can be a meaningless string of events before it ends.

Most of us *hope* we can have a great life. We *hope* for financial well-being, good health and good luck. We *hope* that our children turn out to be productive members of society. We *hope* for peace. We *hope* for the best in life.

Does it make sense to tie one's financial hopes on a lottery ticket? No, it does not but if it were not for the lottery many people would say they have "no hope." The lottery for them is good. On the other hand, if the lottery did not exist, perhaps some of these people would seek alternatives for gaining wealth where their odds of winning could be both higher and more rewarding.

[35] Ed Howe (1853-1937). American editor and author.

Winning the lottery represents money...getting rich. That is why everyone keeps buying another ticket even though the odds are stacked against winning. People are looking for that income which will keep coming in year after year, income that they do not have to work to get. This is called *residual income*.

What if you could accomplish the same results as winning the lottery but engineer your odds of success to be ten times or a hundred times better? Would you try it or at least want to know about it? Of course you would. Who wouldn't!

When you are successful at *Income Surfing*, you also have a chance to create your own lottery-style residual income. How? You focus your multiple income base on things that make residual payouts to you. If you can concentrate your time and effort on opportunities that allow you to receive residual income tomorrow from efforts you put in today, you will accomplish a goal that eludes most people.

Here is another way to look at residual incomes. Suppose your boss told you that the company just created a special incentive program that would take away five minutes of pay every hour you worked, but would accumulate all those minutes in an account that would pay you for the rest of your life. You are giving up one-twelfth of your income each hour. What would you say? Yes? No?

Let us look at the numbers in Figure 8 on the next page.

Figure 8. Example of Possible Residual Income for the Average Worker

Let us assume a worker works a 40-hour work week at $8.00 per hour. Five minutes per hour is set aside as residual income. Forty hours times five minutes = 200 minutes a week.

Assume the worker works 50 weeks a year. Fifty times 200 minutes = 10,000 minutes a year to set aside as residual income.

Remember, you earn on average $8.00 per hour. Five minutes equals one-twelfth of an hour, or sixty-six cents that you are giving up each hour. This breaks down to 13.3 cents per minute.

Your residual income then would be 10,000 minutes x 13.3 cents = $1,333 per year. This money will come in every year *forever* whether you work for the company or not. In other words you will be *vested* in the time set aside each hour you have worked.

Residual Income You Have Earned

After 10 years, $13,000 per year
After 20 years, $26,000 per year
After 30 years, $39,000 per year

Let us look at the power of residual income. At $8.00 per hour for a 40-hour week times 50 weeks per year, the total annual income is $16,000. Without the residual, you must keep working to receive this income, even after 30 years. If you stop working, your income stops, too. By setting a small portion aside each year the *yearly residual income* after 30 years above is 2.4 times bigger *without* working!

According to Figure 8, the higher your earnings, the higher your residual income will be, all things being equal.

Are there companies that offer such a residual income program? We do not know but it sure would be a major boost for workers. You may think that a retirement or pension fund does the same thing, but does it really? The above residual income program pays you every year *regardless of age*. Most retirement or pension programs pay you when you reach a certain age like the late fifties to mid-sixties—ages when you may or may not still have the benefit of enjoying your income. These programs invest your money for you and part of the earnings help fund your retirement. However, the bulk of the earnings may go to the fund managers and not benefit you at all.

As an alternative to retirement or pension programs, you could invest your residual income each year: $1,333 invested at an average of 10 percent interest per year will become $9,868 in twenty years, $25,471 in thirty years and $73,050 in forty years. Remember, this is only one year of $1,333 that was invested. If you invested each year's residual income of $1,333 the numbers when compounded become higher and may carry you to multimillionaire status. And, the residual will keep coming in!

In the United States, fewer than 5 percent of people who retire can live without financial assistance from friends, family or the government. This means that 95 percent of all people who retire failed to generate enough residual income for life in their later years.

Residual income comes in many different forms.

- Dividends from stocks and bonds
- Real estate

- Pension plans
- Royalties from books, movies, patents and other registered forms of licenses
- Life insurance
- Savings accounts

With *Income Surfing* you can develop residual income from nontraditional sources. In today's changing world there are more opportunities than ever before to develop residual income sources.

We made a decision many years ago that we would not put any serious effort into something that did not provide us with a *residual income*. It did not matter what it was or how good it looks, we knew it no longer made sense to work an hour and *only* get paid for an hour, or work a day and *only* get paid for a day. In other words, trading time for money on an on-going basis could no longer produce an above average income. The goal of creating residual income was to put us at the point to earn above average income. We could not do this in a traditional job. Remember, as long as you are in a trading situation--your time for someone else's money--the ability for you to achieve above average success and income will be controlled by someone else.

When dealing with special projects or programs, businesses and corporations realize that it is far less costly to work with an independent person who is *not an employee*. Working as an independent person rather than as an hourly or salaried employee gives you more room to negotiate your compensation. In fact, if you are willing to take part of the financial risk or less compensation up front and be paid more on performance and completion, you may be able to negotiate an ongoing residual income based on the success of the work you perform.

An excellent example of how this is being done is the massive movement of companies electing to work through independent sales representatives rather than to hire dedicated employed representatives. Many traditional companies, which used to employ a sales force of salaried and commissioned people to promote their products and services, are now turning to independent representatives. This frees the corporation from paying costly salaries and expensive benefits packages. In addition, it eliminates incurring a major expense every time it needs to get this sales force together. The independent person usually pays his or her own expenses. Our experience is that independent people do a much better job of finding the least costly way to travel when compared to a company or a corporate travel agency.

Today, a company working with independent people can task these people with all the expenses. In trade for the company not covering these costs, the independent person can expect to receive much higher financial compensation than before for work performed. He or she can also expect to receive bonuses based on performance. And, most importantly, the best situations will provide a program to receive ongoing residual incomes based on repeat business.

The situation described above has been used for many years by direct selling companies. Many of these companies use a multilevel or network marketing compensation program. Since the mid-1960s an increasing number of businesses have elected to use some form of network marketing for their products and services. The transition from traditional to nontraditional marketing such as network marketing has not been without its share of problems, however. Lack of knowledge by the general public has made the average person vulnerable to ignorant news media reporters and government regulators. This has caused some public perception problems. These problems are to be expected, especially when extraordinary individual incomes and rapid corporate growth histories are reported that far surpass those of past business eras. There is little doubt that network marketing is the choice of companies with vision. The 21st century will operate on the principles of independent people who are compensated based on performance.

This means that in the coming years there will be an increasing number of companies converting to performance-based compensation or new companies starting up using that system. The opportunities to become a productive force with these companies will increase. Therefore, there will be more chances to negotiate residual incomes.

Today, revolutionary opportunities exist in media, nutrition, telecommunications, automotive, preventive health care and general product distribution. Companies all over the world need a more efficient method of getting their products and services in front of the consumer. General media advertising, in addition to becoming very expensive, is losing its ability to reach a broad market. Direct mail or junk mail is also losing its effectiveness as its quantity increases and people continue the trend of throwing it into the trash can unread.

Figure 9. How We Buy

Word of Mouth	**63%**
Television	**25%**
Print	
Newspaper	**15%**
Magazine	**13%**
Supermarket Ads	**15%**
Celebrity Endorsements	**3%**

Source: Gannett's *USA Weekend*

The true and tested king of all marketing is *word of mouth* which is what network marketing is about. It is the driving force behind this revolution in product marketing. Take, for example, the Internet. The excitement over the Internet is not misplaced. It is rapidly gaining acceptance and, to many people, it is both exciting and threatening at the same time. Yet, you can have a fantastic Internet site and if nobody knows it exists, you will not get results. Promoting a web site through word of mouth or networking is what will make the Internet powerful. The bottom line is, therefore, networking. Many companies with Internet web sites are benefiting from the power of network marketing.

Putting your time into an effort that does not produce a residual income will provide only temporary results. In selecting the income sources for *Income Surfing,* set your goals and focus on those situations where a residual income can result. By combining your *Income Surfing* forces into a well-managed machine, you will develop over time an income base that you can leave alone while it continues to provide you with a lifetime income.

In summary, where do you have the greatest odds of winning? Check your choice.

Building a future on -

❒ *Income Surfing?* ❒ Lottery Ticket ?

It is your choice!

If you wait for luck to help you,
you'll have often an empty stomach.
--Ignas Bernstein[36]

[36] Ignas Bernstein *The Forbes Book of Business* Quotations page 545

Chapter 13

PRINCIPLES FOR *INCOME SURFING*

> **We have always found that, if our principles were right, the area over which they were applied did not matter. Size is only a matter of the multiplication table.**
>
> --Henry Ford

For anything to work properly there must be an underlying foundation of basic principles or guidelines. *Income Surfing* is no different. As powerful as *Income Surfing* is in achieving true long-term financial and time independence, it must be learned, practiced and maintained.

The "Characteristics of a Successful Income Surfer" in Figure 10 are the ones we have followed and will continue to follow. Time tested, these principles will give you the solid foundation you need to achieve all the success you will allow yourself to have.

Remember, there is no "magic" with *Income Surfing*. Much of what you will achieve will be totally a result of the time and effort you expend. Remember, one of Stephen Covey's key principles from *The Seven Habits of Highly Effective People* is to "begin with an end in mind."[37]

The *end in mind* with *Income Surfing* should be what you want your life to be like when you are successful. And, being successful should go well beyond financial success. Money should be only a measurement of success, not its only goal. Sure it is fun to have money. It can make life a lot more enjoyable and the journey a lot smoother. Success should include family, determine what you can give back to others, what your role in society will be, reflect your belief in a higher being, use all of your talents and strengths, and be a positive influence on others to achieve their full potential.

Beginning with the end in mind will prevent you from following false signals or from traveling down the wrong road. Developing the characteristics found in Figure 10 will help you reach the end you desire.

(See Figure 10 next page)

[37] Stephen Covey, *The Seven Habits of Highly Effective People*. Simon & Shuster Audio Division, NY.

Figure 10. Characteristics of a Successful *Income Surfer*

Successful people -
Have no fear of failure.
Are creative and cooperative.
Take full responsibility for the results they achieve.
Encourage others.
Never get too technical.
Always have a plan of action.
Always write down their goals.
Stay constantly active.
Learns all aspects of their business.
Do not procrastinate.
Are persistent.
Do not wait to get started.
Do not dwell on problems.
Can withstand criticism.
Have a lot of patience.
See good in everything.
Believe in themselves.
Have no room for discouragement.
Learn to communicate well with others.
Dream big.

It's a lot easier to get to the top when you know where you're going!

--Unknown

Chapter 14

PERSONAL GROWTH

> **Undertake something that is difficult; it will do you good. Unless you try to do something beyond what you have already mastered, you will never grow.**
>
> --Ronald E. Osborn[38]

Personal development is so important that it cannot be overestimated or overemphasized.

Planning your future in a step by step approach may sound impractical for some people but it can be accomplished by most of us. Dr. Robert Schuller, famous for his short quips on life, states that *"inch by inch anything's a cinch."*[39] Taking life in small preplanned steps or small bites is better than attempting giant steps or giant bites.

It is this segmenting ability that makes us believe that *Income Surfing* can be done by anyone who is seriously concerned about his or her future and is willing to put the effort into learning how to do it right.

---

[38] Ronald E. Osborne *The Forbes Book of Business Quotations* page 204

[39] *Taken from Tough Times Never Last But Tough People Do* by Robert H. Schuller, published 1983 by Thomas Nelson, Inc. Nashville, TN.

Figure 11 illustrates the problem that most people experience when working today for something that will be accomplished in the future. We know that the average person will spend more time planning a two-week vacation than planning the future.

Developing a program for personal growth study and the processes of helping others develop their skills are the most profitable investments that anyone can make. The returns on the gains from this type of personal investment consistently exceed capital investments by more than two to one. What this means, for example, is that if you have a choice between investing $200 for a book and tape series or attending a self-help lecture *versus* spending the money on a new computer peripheral, *do not buy* the computer peripheral.

Knowledge learned helps, but knowledge learned *and* applied gives you a much better return. A good self-development program not only gives you knowledge, but it also provides you with the direction for the application of that knowledge. It has been said "that man can count the seeds in an apple, but only God can count the apples in a seed." The same will hold true for your ideas. No one knows where they will take you or how much you will accomplish. The only thing known for sure is that without proper personal growth preparation, success will be both elusive and short-lived.

Where are you on the Planning Gap chart? How big is *your* planning gap? Are you growing personally so that you can *accept* the success necessary to reach and enjoy your full potential?

Figure 11. Planning Gap Chart

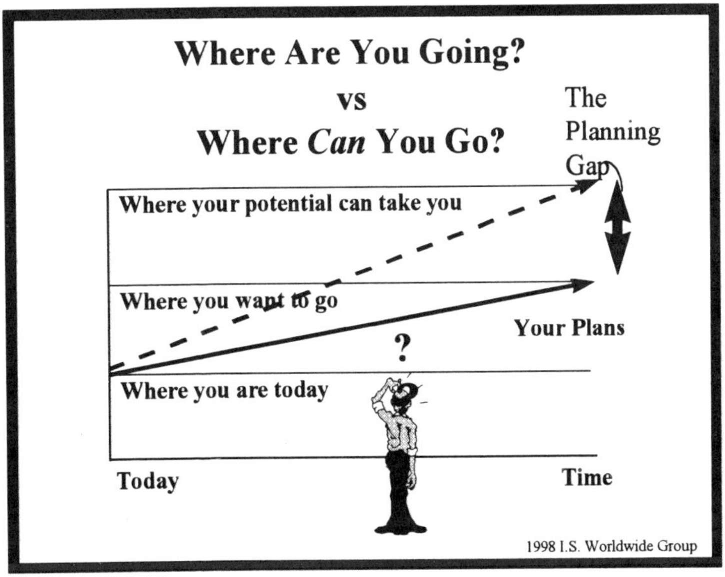

Honesty and hard work are commendable traits of character, but they will never make a success of the person who does not guide them toward a definite major purpose.

--Dr. Napoleon Hill [40]

[40] Hill, Napoleon. *Succeed and Grow Rich Through Persuasion* "Definiteness of Purpose." NY: Penguin Books USA, Inc., 1992, page 224.

Chapter 15

INCOME SURFING AS A TIME MACHINE

Know the true value of time; snatch, seize and enjoy every moment of it. No idleness, no laziness, no procrastination.

--Lord Chesterfield[41]

As you know time is your most precious asset. It is more valuable than money.

In a real sense *time is money* and *money is time*.

Now, we are going to take *time* one step further and tell you that you can make more time for yourself if you choose the correct vehicle or the correct way to make money.

Income Surfing done properly will leverage your time in a fashion that will allow you to accomplish more in a shorter period of time and have more time to enjoy what you accomplish. Does this sound impossible? For some

[41] Lord Chesterfield (1694-1773) English diplomat and writer

traditional workaholics this may appear to be impossible. Others will find it difficult to concentrate on the fact that the traditional time to achieve a particular success can be condensed into a fraction of that time with *Income Surfing*.

Here is an example of what we mean. Let us assume that you are now a fairly good *Income Surfer* and that you have developed and now receive three incomes from three different sources as follows:

Income Source 1--You own a direct sales business for telecommunications services.

Income Source 2--You are a financial consultant to small businesses.

Income Source 3--You write articles for trade publications that require you to meet and interview people in various trades and professions.

You can work at all three sources of income from a home office using common phones lines, a common copier, fax machine and computer, and file cabinets. You may elect to put separate messages on different phone lines. Communications software programs for the computer also provide options for different messages and a mailbox system that you can set up.

The time you devote to each income source is dictated by the priority you give each source. The best method is always to be responsive to income-producing situations immediately and handle administrative functions second. Do not become an organizational guru at the expense of earning money. Without money coming in things can become chaotic very quickly.

Take promotional materials with you wherever you go. Each of your income sources may require a different business card and set of promotional materials. Keep your brief case "loaded" for opportunities that come up. This is especially true when traveling to an appointment for one of your income sources. Along the way you may encounter an opportunity for one of your other income sources, and it will be in your best interest to have materials with you.

However, keep things very simple. Do not go overboard on the promotional materials you carry. The rule is to travel light but with the basics. Your power materials should be for the follow-up or presentation. It is a mistake to load someone up with materials right after you meet them. This is overwhelming and the potential client or customer will probably throw most of it in the circular file. This would waste your valuable money.

As you work your various income sources, the key is to stay organized and manage yourself. You have a responsibility to yourself to be as frugal with your time as possible. Avoid prolonged phone conversations or meetings that are not productive. Do not replace productive time with activity. Activity is when you spend time organizing your files instead of making calls or sending out mailings.

Your time is not your ally when you waste it. Making time your ally is your goal. To do this you must invest it. The best place to invest time is into something that can allow you to leverage it. Leveraging your time simply means that you invest an amount of time into making money so your investment results in an income that continues after you have stopped working.

The general rule for leveraging your time is to invest your time into any endeavor that can lead to repeat or residual business which can result in less work or even no work for the income to continue. Investing time in people can accomplish this. Training a person to do what you do can free up your time to concentrate on getting more business. If the person you train also gets more business, the overall result is more income and more repeat business for everyone. When you train enough good people, you can expect to have your income grow even when you are not working. This is leveraging your time.

John Paul Getty, famous for his success in the oil industry, once said "I would rather have one percent of the efforts of a hundred people than a hundred percent of my own efforts."[42] He knew what leveraging time meant and how important a tool it was in becoming financially independent.

The example incomes discussed earlier can all be worked around each other. There are hundreds of income sources you can select. The key is to build each one to a level where income is coming in all the time. Doing this will ensure you of a positive cash flow and prevent you from having a problem when a single income slows down or stops. Having multiple incomes will also free up more of your time. You win two ways. You have more time and you have more money.

Several years ago a U.S. government agency conducted a study of time management to find out how people use their time to perform various tasks. In the study the same task was given to three different groups of people. The only

---

[42] Poe, Richard. *Wave 3 The New Era In Network Marketing*. Rocklin, CA: Prima Publishing,.1995, page 7.

was given to three different groups of people. The only variable was that each group was given a different amount of time to complete the task. Upon completion the finished task was graded for its quality. Amazingly the group with the least amount of time did as good or better in completing the task than the groups with more time. The group with the most time barely finished within the time allotted.

One conclusion was that people will expand the task to fill the time allowed. Another was that people are basically poor time managers. This is why most corporations implement management systems that require a variety of reports as checkpoints. Unfortunately, many of these systems end up being self-serving and consume much time themselves.

Just because you have a home office or even a small office do not be fooled into thinking that you have plenty of time so you can afford to waste some of it. That is simply not true. It is a danger that will lead to failure.

Leveraging your time through the careful selection of income sources will give you more time and avoid the pitfalls detailed above. It is everyone's goal to live a life of leisure without financial worry. However, this type of life is rare and most likely boring. Would it not be better to remain busy but in control of your time and schedule? You would be more productive and creative, feel more rewarded, have more fun, and attract a more interesting variety of incomes from different sources.

Income Surfing is truly a time machine because it can recover years of standing still where little to nothing had previously been gained. It can accelerate time by speeding up the process to earn money. Many people are learning that they can condense a normal thirty years of earning and saving into a five to ten-year period. In this shorter period people are better stewards of their incomes and find that they can rapidly build financial vehicles that produce excellent ongoing returns.

Look at Figure 12. Assuming a compound total return of 12 percent a year, the average on the Standard and Poors 500 index the past 50 years, here is what it takes to have $1 million at age 65.

Figure 12. How To Become a Millionaire

Age	One-time Investment	or	Monthly Investment
20	$6,098		$59
25	$10,748		$104
35	$33,378		$328
40	$58,823		$594
50	$182,696		$2,121

Source: Liberty Financial Cos.

If Christopher Columbus had invested $1 in an account paying 5 percent a year, upon reaching the New World, his heirs today would have $41 billion, notes Porter Morgan, Chief Investment Strategist at Liberty Financial Company. Obviously, no one has 500 years to let his or her money grow. But "Most of us do have enough time to accumulate substantial wealth if we start investing now and continue investing on a regular basis until retirement." Starting early lets the power of compounding do most of the work while your regular contribution does the rest. Mr. Morgan offers three plans for making a million dollars by age 65. He assumes the money will earn 12 percent a year, not an outlandish rate in today's stock market.

- At age 25, put nothing down but start investing $59 a month.
- At age 40, put $10,000 down and invest $493 a month.
- At age 50, put $50,000 down and invest $1,540 a month.

Even more compelling is the fact that a couple living in 1998 on an income of $50,000 per year would have to have over $1.5 million in savings in addition to social security and pensions when they retire in the year 2008, if they want to maintain the same living style. This is serious! How can the average person save $1.5 million from an income that is just enough to keep pace with his or her present life? It is not possible, unless some type of system exists that can produce above average income in a shorter period of time. The answer is *Income Surfing*, the time machine!

Today, there are many types of businesses that can produce excellent income while allowing you to leverage your time. The best of these businesses are in direct sales and network marketing. Over the past decade more people have become millionaires from direct sales than from any other industry. Set aside any hesitant feelings and start investigating some of these businesses.

The man who wastes his own time may be no less a thief than the man who steals other people's property.

--Napoleon Hill [43]

---

[43] Napoleon Hill, *Succeed and Grow Rich Through Persuasion* NY: Penguin Books USA, Inc.,. 1992, page 257.

Chapter 16

THE SUCCESS PHILOSOPHY OF AN *INCOME SURFER*

The discovery of what is true and the practice of that which is good, are the two most important aims of philosophy.

--Voltaire

All successful *Income Surfer*s must have a *success philosophy*. The tenets of the philosophy should include the following characteristics.

Knowledge

Thoughts are things! They need to be protected and cherished as tools of creation. Whatever you believe, you can achieve. Constantly associate with people and situations that can provide you with new ideas.

Management is essential

Intelligently manage your:

- Goals.
- Money.
- Time.
- Knowledge.
- Associations with other people.

Use your talents, skills, and abilities

Do what you love to do by applying what you know to something worthwhile and rewarding.

Practice the art of being successfully self-employed

If you find yourself bored, listless, or without direction, prepare yourself for a surprise when something may be going wrong. Always have a purpose to your day and for your energy.

Live Uniquely

Copying someone else's success or actions may not give you the same results because of the factors you cannot see. Observe what others are doing to be successful, but be aware of your situation and follow your own instincts.

Read success books

All successes have common threads running though them. They can be found by studying and reading about successful people. Books provide the clues that you can then apply to your own personal situation.

Listen to tapes

Hearing the voice of another person describe how he or she became successful with all the challenges and failures in between can motivate you. Listening to tapes while you are traveling makes the best use of otherwise lost time. Studies of the human mind indicate that the subconscious retains everything you hear around you—both directly and indirectly.

Employ the mastermind principle

We all need the assistance of other people in reaching our goals. Associate with other positive people who believe in you and in what you are attempting to achieve. Seek advice from these people. Avoid people who are negative and pessimistic. Look for people who have the same goals and ambitions that you have. Do not close your mind to criticism, if it is coming from a positive source. A successful mastermind can be two or more people with the same goals and direction.

Be professional

Always conduct yourself in a professional manner. Maintain a good personal appearance and dress according to the respect you would like to receive.

Be flexible

Avoid falling victim to emotional ups and down by being flexible and understanding. Everything moves in cycles.

Be a leader

Follow through on your own ideas and initiatives. Avoid moving with the crowd. Maintain your own standards for integrity and honesty. Separate yourself from those who want to complain without offering a solution or from those who are conducting a "pity party." Leaders maintain a steady pace toward the goal.

Take full responsibility for yourself and your actions

Do not blame others. Avoid inaction or the attitude that someone else will do it.

All distractions are equal

Contain those events that redirect your attention away from your goals. Whether small or large, every distraction has the same result--it either slows you down or stops you altogether. Even the biggest distractions melt in importance over time when compared with attaining a long-term goal.

Overcome the fear of big money

The only thing money cannot buy is poverty! You have an obligation to yourself. Use your talents in a positive manner to earn as much financial reward in your life as possible. Do not compare yourself to others around you. Their life is not your life.

Do not be a perfectionist

There is no such thing as perfection in business or for that matter in life overall. Even the best results can be achieved after failure. An imperfect plan started today is better than a perfect plan started tomorrow.

Invest in service, service and service

Give to others. Help others achieve what they want and you will achieve what you want.

> **It is easy to dodge our responsibilities, but we cannot dodge the consequences of dodging our responsibilities.**
>
> --Sir Josiah Stamp [44]

---

[44] *The Forbes Book of Business Quotations*, page 721, published 1997 by Black Dog & Levanthal Publishers, Inc., New York, NY.

Chapter 17

THE ATTITUDE OF AN *INCOME SURFER*

Nothing can stop the man with the right mental attitude from achieving his goal; nothing on earth can help the man with the wrong mental attitude.

--W. W. Ziege[45]

Eighty percent of all we do in life is based on our attitude. The major difference between success and failure is razor thin, and the majority of this difference is *attitude*.

What is attitude?

- Can you persevere when you know you are right but things are going wrong? If you can, that is attitude.
- Can you remain flexible and compromise without losing

[45] W. W. Ziege *The Forbes Book of Business* Quotations page 80

sight of your goal? If you can, that is attitude.

- Can you be defeated on a major issue--be stopped dead--and regain the energy and desire to try again? If so, you have the right attitude.

Good attitudes come naturally. Bad attitudes are created. A good attitude is something with which you are born. It takes work to develop a bad attitude. A baby is born with a good attitude. Children naturally have good attitudes. Attitudes can be shaped by other people or influenced by outside circumstances. Attitudes come in many shapes and sizes. They can be molded and reshaped.

Regardless of a person's attitude, it is still the individual who has the greatest control over his or her attitude. An attitude can be changed if the person wants to change it. There is no such thing as a *permanent* bad attitude.

As an *Income Surfer* your attitude will be your greatest personal asset. Because you will be on your own, doing something different from the norm, you may be criticized or even ridiculed by people who do not understand what you are doing. These same people may even be jealous of you because you are working on a plan to create your financial independence and become successful.

Figure 13 lists the key attitude characteristics of a great *Income Surfer.*

(See Figure 13 next page)

Figure 13. Attitude Characteristics

I N C O M E S U R F E R

Check ✓ those characteristics you already have.
Work on those you need to develop.

ATTITUDE

- ❒ Faith
- ❒ Belief
- ❒ Be cheerful/optimistic/excited /enthusiastic
- ❒ Committed
- ❒ Accept criticism graciously
- ❒ Welcome problems (challenges)
- ❒ Never become discouraged
- ❒ Do not fear failure
- ❒ Never worry
- ❒ Be thankful
- ❒ Remain teachable
- ❒ Take risks
- ❒ Be flexible
- ❒ Listen
- ❒ Have fun daily
- ❒ Sell yourself!

Chapter 18

THE ACTIVITY OF AN *INCOME SURFER*

To contrive is nothing! To construct is something! To produce is everything!
--Capt. Edward V. Rickenbacker [46]

A common trap for people working on their own is to mistake *activity* for *productivity*. There is a distinct and very important difference in the two.

Activity can be defined as something that keeps you busy like organizing your files. Productivity can be defined as something that produces real results like lunching with a friend to finalize plans for a business project or to obtain a referral for making a presentation about your business.

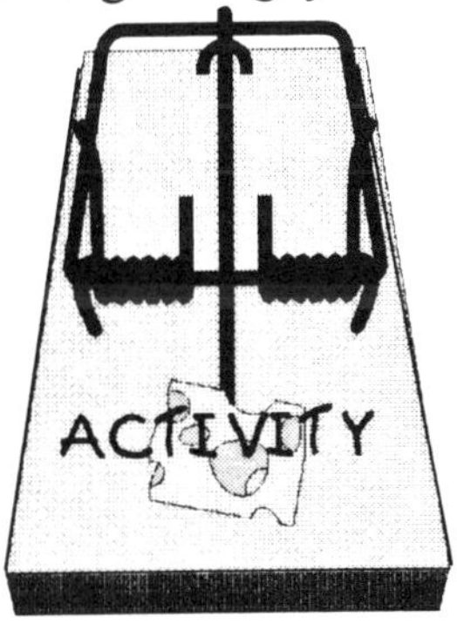

Productivity produces income or potential income. For example, making phones calls to existing or perspective customers is productivity. Sending letters to

[46] Edward V. Rickenbacker (1890-1973) American aviator and airline executive.

qualified prospects, making a presentation to a client, exhibiting your products at a trade show, taking an order or receiving payment for your goods and services is productivity.

Never substitute activity for productivity.

However there are activities that are both realistic and lead to productivity.

The activities listed below provide the foundation for all our actions. An activity which fills time with nonproductive work is a "false" activity because it does not lead to the specific goals necessary for long-term success. Initiating the activities below will lead you to the success you desire.

Figure 14. Activities for an *Income Surfer*

- Write short and long term goals. Be flexible.
- Create a business plan for 30, 60, and 90 days, and for one and five years.
- Create a daily method of operation for each day.
- Give yourself thinking and planning time of at least one hour a day alone.
- Discipline yourself. Remember, all distractions are equal.
- Follow KISS. Keep It Simple, Stupid.
- Do not be afraid of work.
- Be persistence and consistent. Obstacles can create opportunities.
- Keep the business momentum moving forward; the money will follow.
- Do not procrastinate. Do it now!

- Learn to Communicate well. Do not assume people know what you want or mean.
- Make decisions. A good decision today is better than a great decision made tomorrow.
- Become a professional prospector. Never go anywhere without business cards.
- Expect positive results. Accept nothing less.
- Share your success. Help others. You gain more from sharing than taking.
- Picture your dream. The mind will drive you toward a picture.
- Visualize your dream.
- See your dream.
- Feel your dream.
- Believe your dream. Make it real.
- Become your dream. Walk the talk.

The *right results* happen when you have the *right activity.*

Chapter 19

GETTING STARTED AS AN *INCOME SURFER*

Don't wait for your ship to come in; swim out to it.

--Anonymous

Now that you know how to *Income Surf*, let us get started.

We assume you will start part-time and that you will have a home office. We also assume you aim to reach a point where you can intelligently make a decision about becoming a full-time *Income Surfer*. Obviously this will depend on many factors, but most likely your decision will focus on the money you can make as an *Income Surfer*. If your part-time income begins to exceed your full-time income, and you do not enjoy your full-time occupation, the decision may be easy. However, you may be enjoying your occupation and may want to keep your *Income Surfing* part-time. You make the choice.

STEP ONE. Pick your business

Find a business which you can feel comfortable in promoting. Do not attempt to promote something in which you truly cannot believe.

STEP TWO. Determine your time

Once you have identified the products or services you want to promote, you need to determine how much time per week you will devote to them. This is a very important *second step*. Determining time available will dictate the results you can expect to achieve. In the beginning, your results will not be proportional to the time you invest. The opposite will be true. It will look like you are not getting a return, or it will seem very small. Do not be fooled by this. Your goal is not to be an overnight success. It is to build long-term momentum .

Someone once said, "Stove give me heat and I'll put the wood in." If this worked we would all be millionaires without working. Your early efforts in any venture are to "prime the pump." It is only after properly getting started that you can expect to see results. And, it is only after you have established momentum that you can expect to see *measurable* results or financial return. *Money,* is therefore, a form of measurement not a goal of success.

STEP THREE. Develop a DMO

Now that you have determined your direction and have established your time available, the *third step* is to develop a Daily Method of Operation (DMO). The DMO will be your day-to-day guide, a to do list. Your DMO will be done every day no matter what else happens. It will be this consistent effort that will establish the momentum which will lead to financial reward.

A typical part-time DMO should include both prospecting or finding new customers and follow-up or contacting existing customers and prospects. Always maintain a proactive effort to build your business. Never relax or rely on what is already there. This is dangerous. You can be fooled into thinking you have it made only to find out things did not happen the way they were supposed to.

If you are in a people-oriented business, you will rapidly realize that most people do not do as they say they will do. You do not have to become a cynic, just a realist, to know that when someone promises to do something such as place an order, it is up to you to make sure it gets done. If that order or proposal or payment were critical to accomplishing your deadline or meeting your goal, you would lose momentum if it were not accomplished. Take responsibility for making things happen, and learn to identify and rely on others who are also reliable.

Nothing is worse than to be on your own with a limited cash flow. Any income becomes even more important and delays in receiving it can be very troublesome, if not disastrous especially if it was promised and not sent. Big business can absorb problems like this but you cannot. On the other hand, proper planning and smart anticipation can avoid most of these situations. If you have a sense that something may be delayed or is not happening in the proper manner, speak up and voice your concern to your contact person.

As you move forward with your DMO, be flexible in changing it. Not everything is going to work all the time. Do not fall in love with an idea just because it is yours. When you have given your plan enough time to work and you feel like it is not working, make changes. But, do not make big changes, only small ones. Small corrections allow you to measure their effectiveness. Large corrections cause you to lose sight of where you are and make it difficult to determine if your correction was right or wrong.

Some DMOs revolve around numbers. For example, if you knew that 50 percent of everyone you talked to would buy your service or product and you also knew you needed to have two sales per day to make your business work, how many people would you need to talk to each day? The answer is four. This is why you have a DMO. It allows you to gear your energy and time to productive actions that can give you predictable results.

The DMO helps you avoid falling into traps that eat away at your time. There is no money in watching TV!

If you want to enjoy the good life which can come from building residual income through *Income Surfing*, you *must* do what unsuccessful people *refuse* to do. Working hard for a short time beats working hard for a lifetime.

Dr. Napoleon Hill was commissioned in the mid-1930s by Andrew Carnegie to interview the most successful people of the time. After interviewing and studying 500 people, Hill had enough material to write the book *Think & Grow Rich*. This book has become the all-time classic success thinking book and is primarily responsible for the understanding used today to reach success goals. In another book titled *Succeed and Grow Rich Through Persuasion,* Hill detailed those characteristics most common to successful people. He listed seventeen major principles for success that each person he studied followed. To highlight how important having a DMO is to your success, a DMO incorporates five of these seventeen as follows:

1. Personal initiative
2. Positive mental attitude
3. Self discipline
4. Concentration or controlled attention
5. Budgeting time and money[47]

Each person will have a different DMO based on goals, time available and desire to succeed. It should be clear that without a DMO, serious success of any kind will be scarce. Even if it does occur, it will be short-lived. A DMO is necessary to build momentum when long-term success is the goal.

The other twelve principles worked together with the previous five are extremely powerful. They are:

1. Definiteness of purpose
2. Mastermind
3. Applied faith
4. Going the extra mile
5. Pleasing personality
6. Enthusiasm
7. Accurate thinking
8. Learning from adversity and defeat
9. Cooperation
10. Creative vision and imagination
11. Maintenance of sound health
12. Law of cosmic habit force[48]

Make it your priority to read both *Think & Grow Rich* and *Succeed and Grow Rich Through Persuasion* as soon as

---

[47] Napoleon Hill, *Succeed and Grow Rich Through Persuasion,* NY: Penguin Books USA, Inc.,. 1992, page78

[48] Ibid

possible for a full understanding of how these principles are related and why they are so powerful. Many very successful people have given testimony to the fact that it was the reading of *Think & Grow Rich* which provided them with the foundation for their success.

Every adversity every failure and every heartache carries with it the Seed of an equivalent or a greater Benefit.

--Napoleon Hill[49]

[49] Quote from book *Think & Grow Rich* by Napoleon Hill, page 74

Chapter 20

IGNORANCE IS BLISS AND KNOWLEDGE IS POWER

> **When I was a boy of fourteen, my father was so ignorant I could hardly stand to have the old man around. But when I got to be twenty-one, I was astonished at how much the old man had learned in seven years.**
>
> --Mark Twain

How many of you can relate to this quote from Mark Twain? Is it not human nature to think we know more than we really do only to find out later we know less than we think we know?

To some *Income Surfing* will be an exciting new frontier. To others it may seem like a variation of something you may already be doing. Still others will dismiss it entirely. Regardless of your thoughts on *Income Surfing*, you need to experience it if you really want to know what it is. Our goal is for as many readers as possible to understand the power you can enjoy from building a multiple source income base.

So powerful is *Income Surfing* that we believe that the great wealth of the 21st century will in no small way be achieved by people who become experts at *Income Surfing*.

Some of you will be like Mark Twain when he was fourteen-years-old. You will want to shoot off and get *Income Surfing* going right away. Some of you are going to do it your way, what you think is the better way. Try it if you must. But, three, five or ten years from now, are you willing to take the risk that you know what you are doing today and that you will be successful at it? Five years from now is a long time in the business world especially when timing is involved. Are you willing to risk losing today's timing by doing something wrong? Or are you ready to do things right the first time when the opportunity is at its best timing?

Emphasis again must be placed on getting your *Income Surfing* philosophy started now. The experience you will gain by starting simply and then gradually progressing will be far more valuable than waiting until you know everything. With our help and the help of other *Income Surfers*, you will have the best of both worlds--you will be earning while you are learning.

> **If a man empties his purse into his head, no one can take it away from him. An investment in knowledge always pays the best interest.**
>
> --Benjamin Franklin

Chapter 21

INCOME SURFER CHECKLIST

The world is moving so fast now-a-days that the man who says it can't be done is generally interrupted by someone doing it.
--Elbert Hubbard [50]

Income Surfing is very powerful. Like other things worth doing, it is worth doing right.

The checklist of key points in Figure 15 will help you get started. Much like a pilot would use a checklist to help get his or her aircraft through preflight then into flight, we believe that a checklist is the best way to start even though you may already employ some items on the list.

Directions: Check off or fill in the blanks as indicated.

Figure 15. *Income Surfing* Checklist

TIME

Evaluate and indicate how much time you have to dedicate to your new venture.

Part Time ____ No. Hours ______/wk
Full Time ______

[50] *The Forbes Book of Business Quotations*, page 213, published 1997 by Black Dog & Levanthal Publishers, Inc., New York, NY.

YOUR RESOURCES

Home Office _____ **Small Office** _____

Space available _______________

Can people meet you there? _____

Note: If it is possible but not feasible to have people meet you in your home office, consider an executive office suite rental by the hour or day; or meet potential clients or prospects at a neutral site such as a restaurant or club.

Office Equipment

Phone - _____

Business line _____ (Not counting Residential)

Number of lines ____ 800/888 # _____

3-way calling ____

Answer machine ____

Voice mail _____

Calling debit cards _____

Low rates: $_____/min.

6 second billing? ____

Fax machine _____

Computer w/modem ______

Internet access _____

Laser printer _____ Other Printer _____

Copier _____

File cabinet ____

Desk/Tables ____

Note: Many people are finding that the traditional desk does not have the flexibility needed in today's office. Folding tables placed end to end or at angles offers a much better solution.

Financial Management

List all your available resources as follows:

Money -

Savings $ _______

Credit $ _______

Cash $ _______

Credit cards $ _______

Checking account _____

One-write checks _____

Accounting software ______

Accept credit cards ______

Line of credit _____ (as backup only)

Administrative

Business name _________________

Business cards _____

Letterhead /envelopes ______

(Can create these in a computer)

Brochures _______

Note: The availability of pre-printed papers combined with a computer and quality printer allows a person to create their own business cards, letterhead/envelopes and brochures or you may have them professionally printed.

Customer tracking system ______

(Use 3x5 cards or computer program)

People: Mentor __________________

Spouse support ____________

Associates ________________

Other ____________________

Business Type

Kind of business:

____

Service___ Products___ Both ___

Knowledge in any of the above? ____

Inventory

How much to start $_________

Goods or products __________

Cash Flow

Minimum you need to live $________/mo.

Business operating budget: $________/mo.

Projected Income

1st 90 days $ ________

6 months $ ________

1st year $ ________

In summary, use the above information checklist to help guide you as you create your office and build your business. Nothing can replace good planning and a realistic understanding of the point you are starting from.

Have fun!

Chapter 22

LEARNING TO RELAX

Leisure is time for doing something useful, and this leisure the diligent man will obtain.

--Benjamin Franklin

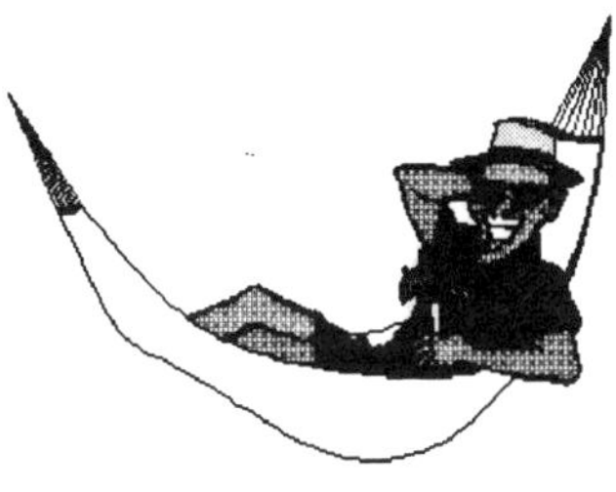

No matter how much fun you are having as an *Income Surfer,* the need to get away from time to time is part of maintaining proper mental and physical health. In addition, relaxation or taking a break will revitalize your thinking and reenergize you. Learning how to relax is an important ingredient for long-term success and enjoyment.

Being on your own carries the weight of being your own best employee. Not having a "boss" to drive you is a major benefit. But, how do you measure yourself when you need to take a break and slow down? This is a challenge. Balancing your personal life with your income-producing life is very important. Listed below are some ideas that we have employed to keep our days fun, exciting and mentally stimulating.

GO FOR A WALK

Just getting out for a walk around the block can work wonders for your energy level. The ability to get fresh air coursing through your lungs will clear up mental fatigue that may have resulted from a session of intense phone work, creating proposals or letter writing.

READ A GOOD BOOK OR MAGAZINE

Invest a half-hour to an hour daily reading a book or magazine. We try to read a variety of magazines every week and at least one good book a month. Setting aside a small portion of our day for this reading helps get this done while allowing for a change of thinking.

GO TO THE MOVIES

It is not uncommon for us to take our spouse to an afternoon movie. We wake up early and work on projects we placed on our "To Do" list from the previous day. By noon we have worked four to five hours. Going to a movie breaks up the day, gets us out for valuable social time with our spouse, and gives us time to mentally relax. After the movie, you can go back to work.

TAKE A DAY TRIP

We have found that having control over our schedule allows us the luxury of going places when other people are working and the crowds are smaller. Instead of going on a crowded weekend, we are able to pick a weekday to visit museums, tourist attractions, and recreation areas.

A PICNIC

Nothing beats taking the time to picnic in the woods or at a park. To break things up, we go to a variety of spots that are easy to get to without taking a lot of travel time. Picking up a sandwich, chicken, or a salad can make it quick and simple.

PARTICIPATE IN SPORTS

There is a wide variety of adult sports opportunities available. Volleyball, softball, soccer, canoeing, running, hockey, basketball and tennis are some sports that have grown in popularity to the point where adult programs are part of every city's or town's recreation schedule. Competitive sports help to reduce tension and change the mind's focus.

JOIN NETWORK ORGANIZATIONS

Getting out to group meetings for education and social interaction is an excellent way to break up the day. Look for breakfasts, luncheons, and business after hours meeting events.

TAKE A MINI-VACATION

Leave on a Friday and come back on a Monday or leave on a Monday and come back on Wednesday. It is your call. *Income Surfing* allows you the freedom to be flexible.

BECOME ACTIVE IN A HOBBY

Join a club that requires outside activity, such as a car club that goes on road rallies to different locations. At the same time network your business to other members or people you meet.

GO TO THE MALL

There is a shopping mall near almost everyone. Take a walk there, window shop, eat an ice cream cone, or buy a pretzel. You do not even have to spend any money, if you just relax and walk.

SIGN UP FOR A COURSE

Most colleges offer extension courses in both the day and evening. Many businesses now offer classes in a variety of subjects for both pleasure and business purposes. Adult extension course are inexpensive ways to learn new skills or enhance interests and hobbies.

Relax and have Fun!!

Chapter 23

BUILDING *REAL* WEALTH

> **Money is power. Every good man and woman ought to strive for power, to do good with it when obtained. I say, get rich, get rich!**
>
> --Russell Herman Conwell[51]

What if you went to work at the age of twenty and woke up one morning at the age of fifty to discover after thirty years that your life savings was a total of $2,300? What would you do? Panic? Cry? Get angry? Give up?

The sad truth is that this is exactly what is happening in America today. The average fifty-year-old has only $2,300 in savings. Even more eye-opening is the fact that the average family has a net worth of less than only $15,500, excluding home equity![52] Another fact is that this is all avoidable with a little education and the application of methods used by people *in the know* for decades. Building wealth does not require making a fortune, nor does it mean winning the lottery. Wealth can be built from ordinary incomes properly invested.

---

[51] Russell Conwell, *Acres of Diamonds Kansas City, MO: Hallmark Editions, 1968*

[52] Merrill Lynch, advertisement, *Wall Street Journal* September 18, 1990.

For example, suppose you had an opportunity to invest $10,000 in a savings account at 24 percent annual percentage rate (APR). What would your account be worth after five years, assuming you made no withdrawals? Your $10,000 would have grown to an amount in excess of $29,000!

At the time of this writing, the typical savings account in a standard U.S. bank pays about 5 percent APR. Putting your $10,000 in an account for five years without withdrawals will earn you just over $2,700. Compared to 24 percent APR, this is a difference of almost $17,000.

Which investment would you choose? People in the know pick the first one. The other ninety-nine plus percent decide on the second.

In addition, what has been called the greatest wealth-building secret--*compounded interest*--can also be applied to our example. Instead of $10,000 at 24 percent for five years, let us carry it out for a total of ten years. After ten years, your account will be worth $118,216! Just look at what compounding has done for you. Likewise, if you invest the same amount at the 5 percent APR rate the amount totals $15,866. Still, which account would you like to have: the one invested at 24 percent APR or the one invested at 5 percent APR?

What you learned in the above examples are only two of hundreds of methods for making your money grow into real wealth. Now that you know, what will you do?

When we first started *Income Surfing,* we knew nothing about wealth accumulation or using the wide variety of methods like the examples shown above. However, as the philosophy of *Income Surfing* became more and more real to us, we started to share it with others. Through this exposure we began to hear from other people who had been practicing the concept of *Income Surfing* without knowing that they were doing it. It was through these people that we learned about the many methods to accumulate wealth. While we would love to share them with you here, there are so many ways of accumulating wealth that the subject has to be reserved for a future book or for one of our seminars.

What we can share here is our sense of urgency that you must start doing things for yourself now. The facts are clear. We are all standing on the precipice of a great canyon where debt and credit have no limits and where there are no warnings to prevent us from falling in. According to data released by the Administrative Office of the U.S. Courts, more Americans filed for bankruptcy in 1997 than any previous year—more than 1.4 million bankruptcy petitions including 1.35 million individuals and 54,000 businesses—a disturbing trend that is climbing each year.[53]

Think of the personal debt and credit crisis as a highway bridge which has collapsed in the night from a freak storm. As each vehicle approaches in the dark, there is no warning to keep it from disappearing over the edge into the black night. One after another each car, truck and bus goes over the edge crashing on top of the one that went before. Finally, one vehicle manages to stop in time, and with its front tires teetering over the edge, its driver is able to warn others to stop. For those where the warning neither came or was too late, it is a catastrophe. To those who were stopped in time, it is a close call and another lesson in life.

---

[53] Press release from *Hartford Courant,* page D2, Feb. 28, 1998. Data from Administrative Office of the U.S. Courts, Washington, D.C.

This financial situation becomes even worse considering that the majority of people do not focus on retirement planning until they are fifty years or older. Assuming that we will continue to live longer means that a man retiring at age sixty-two can expect to live to age eighty-three and a sixty-two-year-old woman will live to the age of ninety.[54] This means that retirement planning must cover a period of over twenty years after all income from wages stops. Even aggressive investing for the twelve years from fifty to sixty-two will fall short of the needed goal. When factoring in inflation, taxes, and possible fund withdrawals for health costs, the picture becomes troublesome.

Assume you are that person at age fifty who is just starting to plan for retirement. What will you do to prevent yourself from becoming totally dependent on relatives or the government? Assume that your relatives are not in the same position or that the government has not already run out of money.

In their book, *Your Life or Your Money*, Joe Domiguez and Vicki Robin talk about "the high cost of making a dying." They site some compelling evidence that everything we have been doing for the past hundred years to get ahead has actually put us in an *upside-down* position.

> You'd think that we'd at least have the traditional symbol of success: money in the bank. Not so. Our savings rate has actually gone down. The savings rate (savings as a percent of disposable income) was 4.5 percent in 1990 (and was as low as 4.1 percent in 1988), whereas in 1973 Americans saved an

[54] Kerry Hannon, "Your Money- Retirement blunders spoil fruits of labor," *USA Today,* January 6, 1998.

average of 8.6 percent. The Japanese, by the way, save over 15 percent of their disposable income.

Not only are we saving less, but our level of debt has gone up--way up. Consumer debt exceeded $735 billion in 1990 (that's 42 percent more than in 1985 and 146 percent more than in 1980). That's $3,000 for every man, woman and child in the country. Every eight seconds a baby is welcomed into our society with a big "Howdy, you owe us $3,000"-- and that figure does not even count the newcomer's share of the *national* debt.[55]

Income Surfing is a way to make more money, but it is also *a way to keep more* while enjoying the trip along the way. Start today on a planned program for savings and investment. It does not matter what your present financial position is or how far you are already in debt. What matters is what you do now to change your future.

Having multiple sources of income will greatly dampen the trauma of losing one of those sources. More importantly, it will allow you to continue your strategy of investment for your future. How many times has someone lost a job, started a business, had a health challenge, or wanted to help another person by using the funds from a retirement account to do so? Plenty of times. Once that money is tapped it is gone forever and so is all the financial power which comes from its compounding.

---

[55] Joe Dominguez and Vicki Robin. "What Do We Have to Show for It?" *Your Money or Your Life,* NY: Penquin Book USA, Inc., 1992 page 6.

Most experts say you should figure on at least 80 percent of your income at the time you stop working (and 100% isn't unreasonable), multiplied by the number of years you expect to spend in retirement.[56] How much will you need-- $500,000, $1,000,000 or $2,000,000? It all depends on your lifestyle, but one thing is for sure: most people greatly underestimate what their financial needs will be.

Since 1980, 5 percent of the U.S. population has become richer while the other 95 percent watched and got poorer. According to Thomas J. Stanley and William D. Danko, authors of *The Millionaire Next Door*, today's rich are not overpaid basketball and rock stars, not corporate managers with "golden parachutes," and definitely not those who fall into inheritances. The rich of today are more than likely people who look dull with a *normal* looking lifestyle, such as "welding contractors, auctioneers, rice farmers, owners of mobile home parks, pest controllers, coin and stamp dealers, and paving contractors." Twenty percent of these are retired and two-thirds of the rest are self-employed. Even more surprising is the fact that the overall median income for this group is $131,000 per year. [57]

There are about 3.5 million millionaire households in the U.S. that include about eight to nine million people. This group represents the top 3.5 percent of the country in terms of household net worth and accounts for more than one-half of the nation's personal wealth. Even this elite group is not classified as true "rich" or even "wealthy" because almost 70 percent of what they earn comes from employment or a self-employed business or profession. What then is wealthy?

---

[56] Kerry Hannon "Your Money- Retirement blunders spoil fruits of labor" *USA Today,* January 6, 1998

[57] Thomas J. Stanley and William D. Danko *The Millionaire Next Door*. Marietta, GA: Longstreet Press, Inc., 1996 Page 9

In his book, *Money: Who Has How Much and Why*, Andrew Hacker defines a wealthy person as someone with any income of at least $1 million. According to the last IRS census there are just over 68,000 people with this income.

Who are the rich in America? In his book, Hacker defines them as follows: "Most of the rich are largely unknown to the public. Many are owners of small enterprises, which sometimes employ fewer than a hundred people. In more than a few cases, these small-business owners live in towns and smaller cities, where they hold leading positions in the local economy."[58] What this means is that to be a millionaire does not mean living like an NBA star, or building a "$2 million vacation home on Nantucket (that lovely island where one day last summer air traffic, almost exclusively from private jets, exceeded that at Boston's Logan airport)." Nor does it mean owning one of the yachts lining Palm Beach harbor in Florida.

Wealth in the 21st century will not be conspicuous, nor will it be ostentatious. It will be a simple, more quiet wealth which can work behind the scenes to do good whose influence can effect a more positive outcome in people's behavior and social habits.

The foundation for this new wealth is being laid now, at the beginning of the 21st century--a period which in historical terms may be the greatest time of wealth redistribution in modern history. Who will be the new wealthy? Obviously,

[58] Hacker, Andrew. Money: Who Has How Much and Why. NY: Scribner, 1997

there will always be the tiny elite group of people who create or foster ideas that affect the masses and who are able to rapidly ride their own momentum to success. We need these people--the inventors, the visionaries, and those people with extraordinary will power and perseverance. But, a larger second group, perhaps even more influential, will be those people who harness the power of building multiple source incomes, who become *Income Surfer*s. They are and will continue to be distributors of information, forming a global network tied together through networking. They will use the new merger of technology and telecommunications to bring an electronic signal to the most modern as well as the remote places on earth. This second group will have the most influence on our direction as a people, and it will be through their focused work that the masses, the 80 percent, will be influenced.

You could become a millionaire if you start practicing wealth-building principles today. The choice has never been clearer. You could be that person who "walks softly but carries a big stick," the person earning income whether you work or not. Now is the time to seize control of your life.

Chapter 24

CHANGING THE WORLD - *NOW*

If you share a good idea long enough, it will eventually fall on good people.
--Jim Rohn

Have you ever stopped to think about *NOW*--that tiny slice of time sandwiched in between the past and the future? As an *Income Surfer* you will have the luxury of using your *now* to its maximum.

Most success thinkers, those people who are truly goal-oriented and who always have a positive mental attitude, will tell you that the number one failure trait for a person is *procrastination,* the failure to act or follow through. The difference between success and failure might only be a split-second decision to do or not to do something. The ability to act *now* has proven time after time to be the major separator between those who succeed and those who fail.

The importance of acting on an idea *immediately* cannot be underestimated. Just imagine if Thomas Edison had thought about creating a light bulb, had envisioned it to the extent that he could transfer his vision to paper, *but* then never took action to actually create it. What would have happened? Nothing. We would all still be in the dark. How about Charles Lindbergh, the first person to fly an airplane solo across the Atlantic Ocean? What if he had only dreamed about it? Where would his life's direction have gone if he had not made the trip? Would we have a global aviation transportation system like we do today? Lindbergh took the risk and proved that long-distance flying could be successful. His actions made the difference. Did you know that the second person to fly solo across the Atlantic Ocean did it faster and used less fuel? This was Bert Hinkler. "Bert who?" you may ask. That is the point. If Lindbergh had hesitated, we might never have known his name. Who was the third person to solo across the Atlantic? It was Amelia Earhart whom we know and remember because she was the *first woman* to make the crossing. She took action and because of that her name now lives on in history.

If you embrace the philosophy of *Income Surfing* for building multiple sources of incomes, you will be making the maximum use of your *now*. Perhaps, not everything you will attempt will succeed, but the fact that you acted will help you grow into something else that might not have previously been possible. Because *Income Surfing* allows you to make maximum use of your skills and talents, it so powerful and timely. Never before in history have we as a people been so challenged to maximize our brief time on the planet earth. Contrary to what the uninitiated may think, *your* ability to produce more results from a block of time using *Income Surfing* is also the power that frees you as the *Income Surfer* to have a fuller and richer life.

Life is full of challenges, and many involve finances. Yet as discussed earlier, money is only number sixteen on the list of life's biggest challenges (see Chapter 1, Figure 1). So, why do so many people use the lack of money to lead lives that are unfulfilled, unrewarding and boring? The answer is fear of losing what they already have. Even though it is less than what they need, fear is keeping them frozen in an occupation or business they hate. If you want a fuller more rewarding life, it is certainly a lot easier with money. However, money by itself is not the answer. Relying on one income source to provide everything you need for a happy and rewarding life has proven to be ineffective for most people. We know that there are many happy and prosperous people dedicated to a single career or occupation which is making them more money than they can count. But, we are referring to average people who go to work everyday. They count the hours before they can go home, count the days before the weekend comes again, and count the months before vacation. Life passes them by because they feel unfulfilled and without direction; they are afraid to attempt something new.

One major result of *Income Surfing* is the challenge to get the most out of life--to do what you feel good at doing. *Income Surfers* can feel the exhilaration of accomplishment when they succeed beyond the average. But, even more importantly, they have an opportunity to make changes in the world around them at a time when that world is struggling with its identity. People all around us need to get their self-esteem back. They need to feel the emotions that result from personal achievement and independence. They need to be recognized for accomplishments that go beyond mere existence. In the book, *Your Life or Your Money*, the authors say:

> We aren't making a living, we're making a dying. For so many working people, however, from people who love their work to those who barely tolerate their jobs, there seems to be no real choice between

> their money and their lives. What they do for money dominates their waking hours, and life is what can be fit into scant remaining time.[59]

The authors go further to make a compelling point.

> Even those of us who like our jobs and feel we're making a contribution can recognize that there is a larger arena we could enjoy, one that is beyond the world of nine-to-five: the fulfillment that would come from doing work we love with no limitations or restraints--and no fear of getting fired and joining the ranks of the unemployed. How many times do we think or say, "I would do it this way if I could, but the board members/Zilch Foundation want it done their way"? How much have we had to compromise our dreams in order to keep our funding or our job? [60]

Is that where we are headed? Will we become people with hollow eyes, experiencing no joy, nor excitement, only burnout? Is this the right way to earn a living?

One of the most far-reaching trends started in the 1980s and 1990s was that of people moving into a home office. This trend is changing industry worldwide. It is also changing families. Working from home not only offers a unique opportunity to regain one's self-reliance and rekindle creative thinking, but it also offers a chance to make a positive change in the family. Just imagine the difference between children who grow up never knowing or seeing what their parents do for a living and those children who

---

[59] Joe Dominguez and Vicki Robin. *Your Money or Your Life* page 3.
[60] Ibid page 7.

observe and experience their parents at work. These situations allow the parents to be important role models versus distant third parties for their children.

Income Surfing can make it possible for person to return to the qualities of life that are the most important. It prevents the sterile environment of a traditional all-consuming job from bleaching out the other joys of life. Our experience as *Income Surfer*s has proved to us that we can enhance our relationships with family members and close friends. We are more in control of our lives because we are masters over our schedules. If we want to get up at 5:00 o'clock in the morning to do some work in our pajamas, we can. If we want to work late, we can. If we want to take our spouse to breakfast for a casual and relaxing conversation, we can. If we want to go to a movie in the middle of the day when the prices are discounted, we can. If we want to attend a child's sporting event, band concert, play, or chaperone a school trip, we can. We are in control.

The ability to earn money from multiple sources frees up our time; it does not take it way. Freedom is power. We can change the world by changing ourselves. Letting our lives become richer through accomplishment because we are not wasting precious time trying to get somewhere else can make a huge difference.

In an interview in *Modern Maturity* magazine, Lynne Cheney, the former chairman of the National Endowment for the Humanities (NEH), and wife of former U.S. Secretary of Defense Dick Cheney said:

> ...today's teachers preach that America is imperialistic and racist, don't believe in such concepts as truth or reality, and think the purpose of

> education is to brainwash students. As if that weren't enough, America's students--from grade school through college--are astonishingly ignorant of U.S. history and similarly deficient in reading, writing, and arithmetic.[61]

The evidence of decay has been there for years. Signals that students cannot accurately tell who current world leaders are or who cannot identify past major events and the people who shaped them have been with us for years. The ability to read and write effectively has been dropping to such an extent that corporations must hold special education classes before allowing new employees to start jobs. Math and science scores are dropping so fast in American schools that twelve others countries now rate higher on aptitude tests where once the U.S. was the undisputed leader.[62] This lack of education is not only affecting our children. It is leading to even bigger problems in adults who cannot tell reality from fantasy, who suffer from the paranoia that "everything is a plot," and that government, business and others are out to get them.

What is happening? If the fact that "one out of three 11th graders cannot write a simple paragraph about him or herself"[63] does not scare you, perhaps you need to take a

---

[61] Lynne Cheney "Indictment" *Modern Maturity* magazine January-February 1998, page 51.

[62] Casper Weinberger Commentary *Forbes Magazine*, October 21, 1991

[63] Ibid

moment to look around. We already mentioned the importance of role models, but who are they? Are they overpaid spoiled sports figures who act like everyone owes them a favor? Are they greedy lawyers who squander their client's funds or who file frivolous lawsuits that clog up our legal system? Are they doctors who scheme to defraud insurance companies and overcharge patients? Are they plotting politicians who trade ethics for votes? Are they self-centered entertainers who flaunt extravagant and excessive lifestyles? Are they publishers who promote sensationalism and exploitation through lies and rumors in newspapers and magazines? Are they drug dealers concerned with no one but themselves?

The wrong role models are being promoted. Parents who take the time and make themselves available to their children are the right role models. We do not hear about them because they do not make sensational press. They are not controversial. They do not live lives of decadent excess. Most live ordinary lives.

The role models we want to emulate are those people who have quietly made a change in the world through ideas and businesses that they have created, people who have created thousands of jobs or have donated millions of dollars to help others. Never before has there been a period of time when so much is happening to change our lives. We need to hear about the people making these positive changes.

One powerful way to promote the right role models is already in existence. Launched in 1995, The Peoples Television Network (TPN) has been broadcasting positive information for personal development 24 hours a day. Using the power of digital satellite television, TPN has assembled a powerful faculty comprised of people who are leaders in making positive changes in our world. A child or adult watching the TPN channel cannot come away untouched in a positive growth sense. It is impossible to hear the true stories about life's challenges from these people who experienced and overcame them without being affected.[64] Our children need *real* role models, not those made from fiction or those who are attempting to live fictional lives. We as adults need these role models just as much.

As an *Income Surfer* you can regain control of your life. In so doing, you can help others around you regain control of theirs. There is so much that life offers. Become a role model to your own family. Use all your talents, not just a few. Teach others around you to be open-minded with a positive mental attitude. Do not let the door of enthusiasm, excitement and hope close on someone who could experience a rich and rewarding life. Help someone else reach their full potential. Together, we have a chance. Together we can change the world.

[64] Information about TPN is available by going to the Internet at www.tpn.com, in writing to TPN 2045 Chenault Drive, Carrollton, TX 75006 or by contacting the I.S. Worldwide Group at 1 800 966-2230

PERSONAL GROWTH LIST

1. Bettger, Frank. *How I Raised Myself from Failure to Success in Selling.* NY: Cornerstone Library Publications, 1949.
2. Brewster, Bob. *Never Sleep Again.* Ellington, CT: Eagle Success Group, 1992.
3. Bristol, Claude. *The Magic of Believing.* NY: Prentice Hall Press, 1985.
4. Conwell, Russell. *Acres of Diamonds.* Kansas City, MO. Hallmark Editions, 1968.
5. Davidson, James & Lord William Reese-Mogg *The Great Reckoning.* NY: Simon & Schuster, 1993.
6. Delmar, Ken. *Winning Moves.* NY: Warner Books, 1986.
7. Dennis, Windsor. *Financially Free.* Dallas, TX: Windward Press, 1990.
8. Domiguez, Joe & Vicki Robin. *Your Money or Your Life.* NY: Penquin Books USA, Inc., 1992.
9. Dunn, David. *Try Giving Yourself Away.* Englewood Cliffs, NJ: Prentice-Hall, 1970 .
10. Edwards, Paul & Sarah. *Making It On Your Own.* NY: Putnam Publishing Group, 1991.
11. Fisher, Mark. *How To Think Like A Millionaire.* Novato, CA.: New World Library, 1997.
12. Hacker, Andrew. Money: *Who Has How Much and Why. NY: Scribner, 1997*
13. *Hill,* Napoleon & W. Clement Stone. *Success Through A Positive Mental Attitude.* NY: Pocket Books, 1977.
14. Hill, Napoleon. *A Year of Growing Rich.*
15. Hill, Napoleon. *Laws of Success.* Chicago, IL: Success Unlimited, 1979.
    --*The Master Key to Riches.* Greenwich, CT: Fawcett Publications, 1965.
    --*Think & Grow Rich.* NY: Ballantine Books, 1988.

16. Hopkins, Tom. *How to Master the Art of Selling.* Scottsdale, AZ: Tom Hopkins International, 1982.
17. Kyne, Peter B. *The Go-Getter*.NY: Henry Holt and Company, 1921.
18. LeBoeuf, Michael. *The Perfect Business.* NY: Fireside Books, 1997.
19. Mandino, Og. *The Choice*. New York: Bantam Audio Publications, 1989.

    --*The Gift of Acabar.* Philadelphia, PA: Lippincott, 1978.

    --*The Greatest Miracle in the World.* NY: Thomas Nelson, 1991.

    --*The Greatest Salesman in the World.* NY: Bantam Books, 1985.

    --*The Greatest Secret in the World Part I and Part II.* NY: Bantam Books, 1989.

    --*The Greatest Success in the World.* NY: W. Morrow, 1983.

    --*The University of Success.* NY: Bantam Books, 1982
20. Murphy, Dr. Joseph. *The Power of Your Subconscious Mind.* Englewood Cliffs, NJ: Prentice-Hall, 1988.
21. Peale, Norman Vincent. *The Power of Positive Thinking.* NY: Doubleday 1990.
22. Poe, Richard. *Wave 3*. Rocklin, CA: Prima Publishing, 1995.
23. Ries, Al & Jack Trout. *The 22 Immutable Laws of Marketing.* NY: HarperCollins Publishers, 1993.
24. Schuller, Dr. Robert. *Move Ahead with Possibility Thinking*. Old Tappen, NJ: F.H. Revell, 1973.
25. Schwartz, Dr. David. *The Magic of Getting What You Want.* NY: W. Morrow 1983.

    --*The Magic of Thinking Big.* NY: Simon & Schuster, Inc., 1971.
26. Scott, Steven K. *A Millionaire's Notebook.* NY: Fireside Books, 1996.

27. Sinetar, Marsha. *Do What You Love, The Money Will Follow.* NY: Dell Publishing, 1987.
28. Stills, Phillip. *Romancing Your Future.* Santa Rosa, CA: Phillip Stills Business Books, 1994.
29. Stone, W. Clement. *The System That Never Fails.* Audio. Los Angeles, CA: Audio Renaissance Tapes, Inc. 1989.
30. Vilas, Donna & Sandy. *Power Networking.* Austin, TX: MountainHarbour Publications, 1992.
31. Waitley, Denis. *The Seeds of Greatness.* NY: Simon & Schuster, Inc. 1983.
32. Ward, Randy. *Winning the Greatest Game of All.* Jennings, OK: Cimarron Management Corp., 1989.
33. Williams, A.L.. *All You Can Do is All You Can Do.* Nashville, TN: Oliver-Nelson Books, 1988.
34. Gingrich, Newt. To Renew America. NY: Harper Collins Publishers, 1995

INDEX

Book Order Form

INCOME SURFING©

Fill in the following information and Mail or Fax to:

THE EAGLE TEAM PUBLISHING GROUP

23 Kibbe Road, Ellington, CT 06029

OR

PHONE ORDERS : 1 800 624-6534

Fax Orders 1 860 870-0524

$ 24.95 U.S Price per copy

$ 3.00 Shipping & Handling Each Copy

$_______ Sales Tax (in CT add 6%)

$ _______ **Total Amount Enclosed**

Canadians please pay in U.S. Dollars

Make Checks (U.S. $) Payable to: ***Eagle Team Publishing***

(Allow 10 days for checks to clear)

For quantity orders fax 1 860 870-0524

Credit Card No. ______________________________

Expiration Date _____/_____/_____

Name on Card(Print) ______________________________

Signature ______________________ Date ____________

Address ______________________________ Apt_______

City______________________ State _____ Zip _______

Phone: Home ________________Office ______________

Watch for the release of an exciting new book coming soon

The *Eagle Team Publishing* Group

Income Surfing©

Reader Response Sheet

Correspond with the authors.
Fax to (860) 870-0524 or
mail to 23 Kibbe Road, Ellington, CT 06029

- We are interested in your comments about *Income Surfing* and any success stories that you want to share with us, especially those stories that utilize the *Income Surfing* philosophy for multiple source incomes.
- If you want to request the authors for a **Seminar** or **Training** to your group, organization, association, or corporation, please detail your request including three (3) alternative dates.

Date ________________

Name ______________________________________

Company ___________________________________

Address ____________________________________

City ______________ **State** ________ **Zip**_______

Phone: **Home** ______________________________

Office ______________________________

Fax ________________________________

Comments or Requests (use additional sheets if necessary):

____

____

Page 2 - **Reader Comments**

____

____

____

____

____

____

____

Signed, ____________________________________

Print name

____

Please ✓ One

❑ Yes ❑ No I also give you permission to use my comments in promotions and other printed matter about *Income Surfing*.

Information about you: Briefly describe your background and occupation:

____

____

INCOME SURFING LECTURE SERIES

The authors regularly conduct motivational lectures and seminars on *Income Surfing.* Their distinct styles and powerful way of relating materials to their audiences make each presentation an unforgettable experience.

Seminars are presented in four-hour or eight-hour blocks.

Fees are based on the seminar type and the total number of people attending. Materials are included in the course fee.

For scheduling information on existing lectures and seminar dates fax requests to 860-870-0524, checkout the web site www.isworldwide.com, e-mail usi/eagle1@isworldwide.com or write to 23 Kibbe Road, Ellington, CT 06029.

Visit the *Income Surfing* web site by going to

www.ISWORLDWIDE.com

INCOME SURFING©

Financial Security in the 21st Century

ABOUT THE AUTHORS

Bob Brewster's (right) professional experience includes military and civilian management training, the founding and operation of several aviation companies, and numerous marketing presentations and proposals. He has piloted all types of helicopters, airplanes, and jets and is a decorated U.S. Army pilot who logged over 250 combat missions in South Vietnam. A graduate of Eastern Connecticut State University, he has worked for large and small corporations. He rose to National Marketing Director with a large direct sales company by building an international sales organization. Bob published a book about his experiences titled *Never Sleep Again* which was sold with much acclaim throughout North America and Europe. A prolific writer, he loves to write about his experiences in hopes that they may help others become more successful.

Ken Norman's (left) professional experience includes several years in forestry management as a procurement forester buying timber for large paper companies, building a successful multiline insurance agency which he sold at a large profit, building a real estate development company, and building and managing a very large and successful 40,000-person international sales organization with a multinational direct sales corporation. A graduate of the University of Florida, Ken spent several years in the U.S. Marines. He enjoys working with people, and his leadership skills have made him a sought after speaker and trainer throughout North America.

Notes:

Notes:

Notes:

Notes:

Notes: